Classic Cocktails

Classic Cocktails

Brian D. Hoefling

A Tiny Folio™
Abbeville Press Publishers
New York London

Project Editor: Lauren Bucca • **Proofreader:** Jennifer Dixon
Design: Misha Beletsky • **Production Manager:** Louise Kurtz

Photography Credits

Mary Ellen Bartley, New York/Abbeville Press: pp. 35, 49, 97, 105, 113, 135, 139, 147, 155, 241, 255; Kenneth Chen, New York/Abbeville Press: pp. 24, 39, 43, 45, 53, 63, 69, 73, 77, 103, 119, 129, 143, 157, 169 and spine, 175, 181, 183, 201, 205, 233, 249; Steve Cohen, New York/Abbeville Press: pp. 2, 31, 57, 61 and back cover, 95 and front cover, 101, 109, 117, 121, 125, 137, 161, 171, 197, 219; Judd Pilossof, New York/Abbeville Press: pp. 55, 87, 151, 187; Alan Richardson, New York/Abbeville Press: pp. 37, 163, 207, 211, 213, 229

First edition
10 9 8 7 6 5 4 3 2 1
ISBN 978-0-7892-1381-5

Library of Congress Cataloging-in-Publication Data
available upon request

For bulk and premium sales and for text adoption procedures, write to Customer Service Manager, Abbeville Press, Inc., 655 Third Avenue, New York, NY 10017, or call 1-800-ARTBOOK.

Visit Abbeville Press online at www.abbeville.com.

Contents

Introduction

There is a kind of magic in a cocktail. The smell of bitters and lemon in a glass can transport you to another time, another place—often one you've never even been to.

A cocktail is an all-encompassing aesthetic experience. The clink of glasses, of ice shuttling back and forth through a shaker. A stunning color gradient settling into the bottom of a Martini glass, a whisper of condensation forming on the outside. The feel of stemware between your fingers, the coldness of the drink against your lips—to say nothing of the exquisite balance of flavors and aromas that cocktails can convey, or their profound power to conjure emotions and memories.

Don the Beachcomber called his drinks "rum rhapsodies" for a reason. Cocktail books have elaborate, flowery titles like *The Bon Vivant's Companion* and *Around the World with Jigger, Beaker, and Flask* for a reason. In cocktails, there is artistry and poetry.

There is also a kind of pervasive mystery. Why else would cocktail names be so evocative, like details from a story you haven't read yet? The Widow's Kiss, the Jasmine, the Lion's Tail—these names inspire wonder and curiosity, and make you want to find out the ending, even if you have to write it yourself.

In this combination of beauty and mystery, there is magic.

You don't need me to give you reasons to appreciate cocktails. I know that because you're reading this book. But I also expect that you won't mind hearing a few more. So let's talk about this captivating art form, and why it brings us so much joy.

People have been mixing alcohol with other beverages since the dawn of civilization. This makes sense: alcohol is great at carrying flavors. The tastes and aromas we enjoy steep much more readily into alcohol than into water or other liquids. When we find a flavor that we want to savor or preserve, we add booze.

It also makes sense because we're human beings. There's a whole universe around us that we experience through our bodies, through our senses, and through our minds. We like variety. We like novelty. We like to play with the world we're in.

And so we've been tinkering with this flavorful intoxicant, and augmenting it with intriguing smells and tastes, for at least six thousand years.

The earliest recorded ancestor of beer came from ancient Sumer, and incorporated date honey in addition to fermented barley. Beer has always been flavored—with a blend of herbs in Medieval Europe, with hops today—while we've been spicing wine since antiquity and infusing spirits since the Renaissance.

Once people had sugar, citrus, and spices in the same place as their wine and liquor, they began combining them into punches. When commercial ice harvesting took off in the nineteenth century, ice became *de rigeur* in mixed drinks. We have never stopped inventing, never stopped iterating, and never failed to incorporate new tools or ingredients into our booze as they became available.

In the United States in the early 1800s, the new ingredient was bitters. Developed (and later discredited) as patent medicines, bitters were highly concentrated macerations of various spices in alcohol. They were also highly flavorful, and American drinkers began adding dashes of them to their recreational alcohol, and by 1806, we had our definition of a cocktail in print: "*Cocktail* . . . is a stimulating liquor, composed of *spirits* of any kind, *sugar*, *water*, and *bitters*—it is vulgarly called *bittered sling*" (Harry Croswell, *The Balance, and Columbian Repository*, May 13, 1806).

Or, in modern parlance, an Old Fashioned with your choice of base spirit. At the time, the cocktail would have been available as one of a menu of fairly simple concoctions—slings, juleps, sours, and so on—which you ordered by naming your spirit and preparation of choice, e.g., a Brandy Cocktail or a Gin Sour.

Over the next two hundred years, the definition of "cocktail" was broadened, first to include all drinks that contained bitters, and then any sort of spirit-forward mixed drink one could take as an aperitif. Today, any sort of alcoholic mixed drink is commonly called a cocktail.

But what all of these drinks have in common, and what indeed they have in common with those early juleps and sours that have since been admitted into the canon, is that they're combinations of *finished products*. When faced with the finest work a distiller can muster, the maker of cocktails says, "I can improve this." It is an expression of that irrepressible urge to play with our food, to reorder the world around us, to experience things that we might not have experienced before. It is also an expression of confidence.

In this, cocktails are like the punches from which they directly descend. Unlike punch, however, cocktails are made to order: for individuals, to suit individual tastes. This is perhaps the great innovation that distinguishes them from all other things in the grand field of mixed and flavored alcoholic beverages: a cocktail is meant to be both the most improved *and* the most custom-tailored experience a drinker can have with a particular bottle.

And is it any wonder that something so cocksure and so individualized came out of the United States of America? The cocktail really, truly, is ours in spirit, born of America's industriousness and ambition, our inventiveness and our disregard for authority, our crotchet and our indulgence.

It took roughly a century for the rest of the world to catch on. The European producers of vermouth and brandy had long found the American habit of *mixing* them strange, even vulgar. But by the end of the nineteenth century, that was beginning to change. As the number and variety of cocktails grew, they began to seem attractive—they were after all modern, and from that exotic land across the sea. European cocktail guides began to be published, and cocktails began to be served outside the United States.

That process was accelerated during the decade-long American experiment in not consuming cocktails (officially), otherwise known as Prohibition. By the 1920s, any international holdouts against the cocktail had to get on board fast, because the Americans who could afford to were going abroad to drink. Soon, the great centers of cocktail making were not New York or Chicago or San Francisco, but London, Paris, and Havana.

However compelling the aesthetics of the Roaring Twenties were, make no mistake: virtually no good drink from that decade was invented in the United States. Speakeasy booze was often bad and recipes were designed to disguise rather than to enhance its flavor. The best thing the Volstead Act did for cocktails was to spread them around the world.

While Prohibition was ultimately repealed, it undercut the cocktail's position for a generation of American drinkers, some of whom had obeyed the law and never tasted one, while others had only tried the foul-tasting, blindness-inducing underground variety. The subsequent privations of the Great Depression and the rationing of the Second World War helped usher in a period of midcentury doldrums, often nicknamed the Cocktail Dark Ages.

People didn't stop drinking during the *Mad Men* era, but they were drinking differently. Preferences tilted towards lighter spirits rather than full-flavored ones—vodka found success in the U.S., while many other distillers promoted the "blandness" of their products—and cocktails began to seem rather, well, old-fashioned. In the age of Campbell's *Cooking with Soup*, most drinks that survived could be made entirely with bottled ingredients: vermouth, bitters, grenadine, lime cordial, and so on. Innovation was rare, and largely confined to the realm of tropical or "exotic" drinks, rather than mainstream cocktailery.

It is ironic, then, how much we owe to this era. Its standard cocktail list—remarkably consistent from the Second World War to the 1990s—summarized two centuries of invention in a few dozen recipes, and is the closest we've come as a society to deciding which drinks are Really Important.

Moreover, the stability of that list laid the groundwork for the Cocktail Renaissance. The bartenders and enthusiasts who were drawn to venerable drinks were mixing Sidecars and Ward Eights and Stingers before they discovered the rest of the iceberg. An explosion of curiosity followed, abetted by the nascent internet communities of the nineties and the aughts, and periodically goosed by the reprinting of an old cocktail book, the revival of a long-forgotten recipe, or the reintroduction of a formerly unavailable product (some of which, like absinthe and orange bitters, are once again considered staples). Across the U.S., and then the world, the cocktail was making a comeback.

The Renaissance was in its full flower when I first encountered it. Weeklong cocktail conferences appeared in various cities, offering education on drinks history, techniques, and spirits production. Out-of-print cocktail guides were suddenly available online or in facsimile editions. Extraordinarily talented bartenders were reviving the unjustly forgotten—the Vieux Carré, the Negroni, the Last Word—and minting new drinks along classical lines, using ingredients like mezcal and elderflower liqueur that their forebears didn't have.

It was a heady time, and it was necessarily a temporary one. After a few decades, the irrepressible urge to innovate took over from the project of revival, and a proliferation of new techniques and ingredients made it possible for bars to make something new nearly every day. The Renaissance also helped reassert the respectability of hospitality as a profession, and even give tending bar a new cachet. In time, the interplay between amateurs and professionals was reduced—in part as folks like me moved from the first group into the second—and what might once have been called the cocktail movement gradually became today's hospitality community.

We are now living after the Renaissance—I've been promoting the term "Cocktail Baroque Period" for three or four years now, albeit with little success—and while there is much to recommend our era I still feel a sense of loss. Where ten or twenty years ago a bar could build a reputation on its Bee's Knees, the markers of Good Cocktail Bars today are more intricate, more Instagrammable, and less reproducible at other bars or at home. I love these drinks and the people who make them, but I worry what this change portends for the field.

The idea of a "classic," that nebulous notion with which this book is titled, presumes a canon of some kind. But there is not and cannot be a final list: there is no certain set of qualities, no group of experts, no vote of the drinking public that can decide what is classic and what is not. It is a mixture of subjective and objective characteristics, assessments of a thing's quality, its popularity, and its influence.

An artistic canon—and the cocktail is surely an artistic medium, an expression of beauty through form and composition—is at its core a dialogue among its practitioners, consumers, and critics. New examples are created while old ones are reassessed, discarded, revived. There will often be agreement about which ones *must* or *cannot* be considered important, but what is most essential is that the discourse continue, that those who care continue to form and express opinions about what lies between "definitely" and "absolutely not." If this dialogue ends, the canon will atrophy; or, to put it plainly, art we don't care enough about will cease to be produced.

The Cocktail Renaissance was the most robust conversation about classic drinks we have yet had, and it has left us an incredible bounty to enjoy. It is simultaneously the case that we are not adding to the canon in the Cocktail Baroque Period, either by invention or by revival, at nearly the rates we were. That makes this an ideal time to take stock, to consider the lessons we wish to draw from the last era and its enduring impact on our conception of the classics. It should also remind us that the magic of cocktails, so beautifully captured in the zeitgeist of the Renaissance, is ephemeral.

I do not mean to leave you on a bleak note. Cocktails are in their strongest position in a hundred years, and the mere existence of this book is evidence of that. But they are a fragile art form, and one we've lost before. If you care about them, make them. Drink them. Share them. Pass them on. I hope this book will help.

A Note on Recipe Selection

As we proceed with this dialogue about which drinks are essential and which ones may not be, here are the guidelines I've used in selecting recipes for this book. As promised, they are neither arbitrary nor objective:

1 It has maintained consistent popularity from the First Cocktail Golden Age (roughly between the 1860s and Prohibition, extending into the 1930s in some places) until today (e.g., the Old Fashioned).

2 It fell out of fashion after the F.C.G.A., but was subsequently revived and enjoys resounding popularity today (e.g., the Negroni).

3 It was historically popular, and while it is less so today, its influence on the canon or on wider culture is undeniable (e.g., the Gimlet).

4 It is so widely known today that it would be absurd to exclude, even if it is of recent vintage or its place in history is not yet guaranteed (e.g., the White Russian).

5 It was not particularly popular during the F.C.G.A., but has been plucked from obscurity to find wide success during the Cocktail Renaissance (e.g., the Last Word).

6 It is a cocktail invented *during* the Cocktail Renaissance that now appears widely on cocktail menus alongside the classics and is regarded as a contemporary classic (or seems likely to become one (e.g., the Penicillin).

7 Other major figures have regarded it as an essential classic drink (e.g., the Jack Rose).

8 Its role in cocktail history is significant enough that it merits inclusion irrespective of its individual popularity (e.g., the Japanese).

9 It is moderately significant by the other standards here listed and I believe it to be a good drink deserving a wider audience (e.g., the Palmetto).

By necessity, not every drink you've heard of will be in here. I insisted—and I can promise you—that every recipe in this book is one I had personally tested and felt was worth drinking. There are cocktails in here I would be unlikely to make or order, but if it's in here, I believe that at least this version of it is a good drink. If it didn't make the cut, I either didn't think it was important enough or didn't believe a good version could be made.

You may disagree with some of my exclusions. If you do, good! Go out and order the drink you feel I've been unfair to. Build up its following. Write a book of your own. Make it a classic.

But whatever you do, keep the conversation going.

Acacia

2 oz. London dry gin
¾ oz. Bénédictine
¼ oz. kirschwasser

Stir with ice and strain into a chilled
cocktail glass. Express a lemon peel
over the glass and drop it in.

Adonis

1½ oz. sherry
1½ oz. sweet vermouth
2 dashes orange bitters

Stir with ice and strain into a chilled cocktail glass. Garnish with an orange peel.

Air Mail

1½ oz. moderately aged rum
¾ oz. lime juice
½ oz. honey
1½ oz. sparkling wine

Shake all but the wine without ice,
then again with ice. Strain into a chilled
cocktail glass. Top with the sparkling
wine and garnish with an orange peel.

Alaska

2 oz. Old Tom gin
1 oz. Yellow Chartreuse
2 dashes orange bitters

Stir with ice. Strain into a chilled
cocktail glass.

Amaretto Sour

1½ oz. amaretto
1 oz. lemon juice
1 tsp. rich demerara syrup

Shake with ice. Strain into a rocks glass
with ice. Optionally, garnish with a
brandied or maraschino cherry.

Contemporary bartender Jeff Morgenthaler claims to make the best Amaretto Sour in the world. He's right. To make his version, add an egg white and ¾ oz. cask-strength bourbon, and shake once without ice before adding ice and shaking again. The foam can optionally be decorated with bitters. The recipe on the facing page is more traditional, but the Morgenthaler version is unbelievably tasty and still recognizably an Amaretto Sour. When serving it, he advises that you "grin like an idiot as your friends freak out."

Americano

1 oz. Campari
1 oz. sweet vermouth
2 oz. seltzer

Combine ingredients in a rocks glass
with ice and stir. Garnish with a lemon
peel.

Applejack Rabbit

1¾ oz. high-proof apple brandy
½ oz. maple syrup
½ oz. lemon juice
¼ oz. orange juice

Shake with ice. Strain into a chilled
cocktail glass.

Army & Navy

1¾ oz. London dry gin
¾ oz. orgeat
½ oz. lemon juice
2 dashes Angostura bitters

Shake with ice. Strain into a chilled cocktail glass.

Aviation

2 oz. London dry gin
¾ oz. lemon juice
½ oz. maraschino liqueur
¼ oz. crème de violette

Shake with ice and double strain
into a chilled cocktail glass. Optionally, garnish with a brandied or
maraschino cherry.

Dusty and neglected for years, the Aviation piqued the interest of cocktail revivalists like Paul Harrington and Ted Haigh. With the discovery of Hugo Ensslin's original recipe using crème de violette, its popularity sky-rocketed. Haus Alpenz brought the liqueur to American shores after decades of unavailability, and the Aviation became the calling card of the mixologically literate. By 2012, with backlash brewing against the Cocktail Renaissance's standard list of drinks, the legendary Dale Degroff was labeling the Aviation "do not resuscitate" and former partisans abandoned it in droves. Robert Simonson argues in *Punch* that it will never disappear, but its brief, dramatic heyday is over.

B & B

1½ oz. brandy
¾ oz. Bénédictine

Combine ingredients in a rocks glass
with ice and stir. Optionally, express a
lemon peel over the glass and discard.

Bamboo

1½ oz. sherry
1½ oz. dry vermouth
1 tsp. rich demerara syrup
1 dash Angostura bitters
1 dash orange bitters

Stir with ice and strain into a chilled
cocktail glass. Express a lemon peel
over the glass and discard.

The Bamboo is often credited to Louis Eppinger, a German emigrant who made a career as a saloon-keeper and hotelier on the Pacific coast of the U.S. until 1890 when he was drafted to take the reins of Yokohama's Grand Hotel; certainly, it was a specialty of his. The Bamboo moved east as Eppinger moved west, crossing the States in the 1880s and '90s, and occasionally being called the "Boston Bamboo" for reasons lost to time. Modern bartenders are increasingly joining Eppinger in adopting it as a signature drink, because its simplicity shows off the bartender's skill in preparation and ingredient selection.

Beachcomber

1½ oz. unaged or filtered
   lightly aged rum
½ oz. curaçao or triple sec
½ oz. lime juice
1 tsp. maraschino liqueur
¼ oz. simple syrup (optional)

Shake with ice and strain into a chilled
cocktail glass. If not using simple
syrup, sugar the rim of the glass first.

Bee's Knees

2 oz. London dry gin
1 oz. lemon juice
¾ oz. honey

Shake without ice, then again with ice.
Strain into a chilled cocktail glass.

Bellini

1½ oz. chilled peach puree
4½ oz. chilled sparkling wine

Pour peach puree into a chilled flute, followed by sparkling wine. Stir to combine. Optionally, garnish with a long, thin twist of lemon.

Bijou

1 oz. London dry gin
1 oz. sweet vermouth
¾ oz. Green Chartreuse
1 dash orange bitters

Stir with ice. Strain into a chilled
cocktail glass. Optionally, garnish with
a brandied or maraschino cherry.

*I*t's often said that each ingredient represents a jewel (*bijou* in French): the Chartreuse is emerald, the vermouth is ruby, and the gin is diamond. Harry Johnson was the first to attach the name to this recipe, although it's unclear whether he invented it. An incredibly influential figure at the turn of the twentieth century and the author of multiple bartender's guides, Johnson also had a penchant for easily debunked exaggerations and the occasional outright lie. His fabrications complicate a legacy otherwise marked by widely recognized skill and professionalism.

Bitter Giuseppe

2 oz. sweet vermouth
¾ oz. Cynar
2 dashes orange bitters
wedge of lemon

Combine vermouth, Cynar, and bitters
in a rocks glass with ice and stir.
Squeeze lemon wedge over the glass
and drop it in.

Black Russian

1½ oz. vodka
¾ oz. coffee liqueur

Combine ingredients in a rocks glass
with ice and stir.

Blinker

2 oz. rye whiskey
1 oz. grapefruit juice
½ oz. grenadine

Shake with ice. Strain into a chilled
cocktail glass.

*For a Dr. Cocktail's Blinker, sometimes
called a Dr. Blinker, substitute ½ oz.
raspberry syrup for the grenadine.*

Blood and Sand

1¼ oz. blended Scotch
¾ oz. sweet vermouth
¾ oz. Cherry Heering
¾ oz. orange juice

Long shake with ice and double strain
into a chilled cocktail glass. Express an
orange peel over the glass and discard.

Bloody Mary

2 oz. vodka
4 oz. tomato juice
½ oz. lemon juice
3 dashes Worcestershire sauce
1 pinch celery salt
1 pinch black pepper
1 tsp. rich demerara syrup (optional)

Roll between two tins with ice. Pour
unstrained into a highball glass with a
salted rim.

Boulevardier

2 oz. bourbon
1 oz. sweet vermouth
1 oz. Campari

Stir with ice and strain into a chilled
cocktail glass. Optionally, garnish with
an orange peel.

Bramble

2 oz. London dry gin
¾ oz. lemon juice
½ oz. simple syrup
½ oz. crème de mûre

Shake gin, lemon juice, and simple syrup with ice. Strain into a rocks glass filled with crushed ice and drizzle crème de mûre on top. Garnish with a slice of lemon and 1–2 blackberries speared on a toothpick.

Brandy Alexander

1 oz. brandy
1 oz. crème de cacao (brown)
1½ oz. light cream or half-and-half

Shake with ice and strain into a chilled
cocktail glass. Garnish with a sprinkle
of grated nutmeg.

Brandy Flip

1½ oz. brandy
½ oz. rich demerara syrup
whole egg

Shake without ice, then again with ice. Strain into a chilled cocktail glass and garnish with a sprinkle of grated nutmeg.

Flips can be made with all kinds of spirits and even fortified wines. You can substitute your favorite rum or whiskey directly for the brandy in this recipe. If using port wine or sherry as the base, you may want to use 2 oz. instead of 1½ oz., and reduce the demerara syrup to ¼ oz.

Bronx

1½ oz. London dry gin
½ oz. sweet vermouth
½ oz. dry vermouth
¾ oz. orange juice

Shake with ice. Strain into a chilled
cocktail glass.

*For an Income Tax, add a dash of
Angostura bitters. For a Queens,
substitute ½ oz. pineapple juice
for the orange juice.*

Caipirinha

2 oz. unaged cachaça
1 lime
2 tsp. sugar

Cut lime into quarters and muddle well
with sugar in a large rocks glass. Add
cachaça and ice and stir.

*E*very rum-producing country has a signature combination of their spirit with lime and a sweetener (e.g., the Daiquiri, Corn 'n' Oil, and Ti' Punch). The same is true of Brazil, although whether cachaça should be considered a rum is a matter of dispute. If "rum" means any spirit distilled from sugarcane, it certainly qualifies; but cachaça producers point to a history wholly separate from Caribbean rums, and cachaça's traditional aging in native Brazilian hardwoods. Either way, it's a rustic drink—the name means "little peasant girl"—so use raw ingredients and don't try to fancy it up.

Cape Codder

1½ oz. vodka
4 oz. cranberry juice cocktail
wedge of lime

Combine vodka and cranberry juice
cocktail in a highball glass with ice and
stir. Squeeze lime wedge over the glass
and drop it in.

Champagne Cocktail

5 oz. chilled Champagne
1 sugar cube
4 dashes Angostura bitters

Place sugar cube in a chilled flute and
soak with bitters. Fill with Champagne.
Stir gently with a barspoon to dissolve
sugar. Express a twist of lemon over
the glass, run it around the rim, and
drop it in.

Chartreuse Swizzle

1½ oz. Green Chartreuse
1 oz. pineapple juice
¾ oz. lime juice
½ oz. falernum

Swizzle with crushed ice in a highball glass. Garnish with a sprig of mint and a sprinkle of grated nutmeg.

Chrysanthemum

2 oz. dry vermouth
¾ oz. Bénédictine
1 tsp. absinthe

Stir with ice and strain into a chilled cocktail glass. Express an orange peel over the glass and discard.

Clover Club

1½ oz. London dry gin
½ oz. dry vermouth
½ oz. lemon juice
½ oz. raspberry syrup
egg white

Shake without ice, then again with
ice. Strain into a chilled cocktail
glass. Optionally, garnish with 2–3
raspberries speared on a toothpick.

Julie Reiner, an early leader of the Cocktail Renaissance and proprietor of the Brooklyn bar Clover Club, has sensibly pointed out that if you're going to name your bar after a cocktail, it should be one almost everybody will enjoy. In consultation with her friend and neighbor, cocktail historian David Wondrich, she developed a house version true to the earliest-known recipe for the drink, incorporating a forgotten slug of dry vermouth and restoring the raspberry syrup that had long been displaced by grenadine. No longer a near-clone of the Pink Lady, this new-old Clover Club stands as one of the greatest beneficiaries of mixological archaeology.

Coffee Cocktail

2 oz. ruby port
1 oz. brandy
1 tsp. sugar
whole egg

Shake without ice, then again with
ice. Strain into a chilled cocktail glass
and garnish with a sprinkle of grated
nutmeg.

Corn 'n' Oil

2 oz. moderately aged rum
½ oz. falernum
2 dashes Angostura bitters
wedge of lime

Swizzle rum, falernum, and bitters
with crushed ice in a rocks glass.
Squeeze lime wedge over the glass and
drop it in.

Two questions bedevil the Corn 'n' Oil: why is it called that, and should there be lime juice in it? The name is often said to refer to an oil-slick-like float of black rum, but this is nonsense, according to Barbadian distiller Richard Seale, because the drink was originally made with brandy. Seale believes it alludes to Deuteronomy 18:4, which grants the priests the firstfruits of "thy corn . . . and thine oil"; and that rum replaced the brandy around World War I. As for the lime, the best sources I have disagree, so garnish with a wedge and squeeze to taste!

Corpse Reviver No. 1

2 oz. brandy
1 oz. apple brandy
1 oz. sweet vermouth

Stir with ice. Strain into a chilled
cocktail glass.

Corpse Reviver No. 2

¾ oz. London dry gin
¾ oz. curaçao or triple sec
¾ oz. Kina apéritif wine
¾ oz. lemon juice
1 tsp. absinthe (rinse)

Shake first four ingredients with ice.
Strain into a chilled cocktail glass
rinsed with absinthe.

Cosmopolitan

2 oz. lemon vodka
1 oz. curaçao or triple sec
1 oz. cranberry juice cocktail
1 oz. lime juice

Shake with ice and strain into a chilled
cocktail glass. Express a lemon peel
over the glass and discard.

Cuba Libre

2 oz. lightly aged rum
4 oz. cola
wedge of lime

Combine rum and cola in a highball
or rocks glass and stir. Squeeze lime
wedge over the glass and drop it in.

Daiquiri

2 oz. rum
¾ oz. lime juice
¾ oz. simple syrup

Shake with crushed ice, or long shake
with cubed ice. Double strain into
a chilled cocktail glass. Optionally,
garnish with a lime wheel.

*The most traditional rum for a Daiquiri
would be a lightly aged and filtered
"white" rum in the Cuban or Puerto
Rican style, but no rum worth drinking
will make a bad Daiquiri. Personally,
I prefer it with unaged rums.*

De La Louisiane

1½ oz. rye whiskey
¾ oz. sweet vermouth
¾ oz. Bénédictine
3 dashes Peychaud's Bitters
1 tsp. absinthe (rinse)

Stir first four ingredients with ice.
Strain into a chilled cocktail glass
rinsed with absinthe.

*Also known as La Louisiane, À La
Louisiane, Cocktail à la Louisiane,
and so on.*

Death in the Afternoon

1½ oz. absinthe
4 oz. sparkling wine

Pour absinthe into a chilled flute,
followed by sparkling wine. Stir gently
to combine.

Deep Blue Sea

2 oz. London dry gin
¾ oz. Kina apéritif wine
¼ oz. crème de violette
2 dashes orange bitters

Stir with ice and strain into a chilled
cocktail glass. Express a lemon peel
over the glass and discard.

Diamondback

1½ oz. high-proof rye whiskey
¾ oz. apple brandy
¾ oz. Yellow Chartreuse

Shake with ice. Strain into a chilled
cocktail glass. Optionally, garnish with
a brandied or maraschino cherry.

Division Bell

1 oz. mezcal
¾ oz. Aperol
¾ oz. lime juice
½ oz. maraschino liqueur

Shake with ice. Strain into a chilled
cocktail glass. Optionally, garnish with
an orange or grapefruit peel.

Earthquake

2½ oz. brandy
¼ oz. absinthe

Combine ingredients in a rocks glass
and stir without ice. Express a lemon
peel over the glass and discard.

There are several noteworthy drinks invented by writers, but the Earthquake stands alone as the creation of a painter: Henri de Toulouse-Lautrec, famous for his depictions of (and life among) the Parisian demimonde in the Belle Epoque. Lautrec had a fondness for cuisine, for the elaborate, and for absinthe. His parties were decadent and dangerous.

Lautrec's original, evocatively called the *Tremblement de Terre* in French, called for equal parts Cognac and absinthe, mixed and served at room temperature. This recipe is a modern interpretation, less lethal and more palatable for the rest of us.

Egg Nog

12 eggs · ¾ cup sugar · 1 pint brandy
½ pint moderately aged rum
1 pint milk · ½ pint heavy cream
nutmeg

Separate eggs. Beat yolks in a large
serving bowl, adding sugar a little at a
time and continuing until all is dissolved.
Continue stirring mixture and slowly
pour in brandy, then rum. Repeat
with the milk and then the cream. In a
separate bowl, beat the egg whites until
stiff, then fold into the mixture and stir
in grated nutmeg to taste. Chill before
serving and top each glass with a sprinkle
of grated nutmeg. Keeps for several days
if refrigerated.

El Presidente

1½ oz. filtered lightly aged rum
1½ oz. blanc vermouth
1 tsp. curaçao or triple sec
1 tsp. grenadine

Stir with ice and strain into a chilled cocktail glass. Express an orange peel over the glass and discard.

Florodora

1½ oz. London dry gin
½ oz. lime juice
⅓ oz. raspberry syrup
4 oz. ginger ale

Combine gin, lime, and raspberry
syrup in a highball glass with ice
and stir. Fill with ginger ale.

Fog Cutter

1½ oz. lightly aged rum
½ oz. brandy
½ oz. London dry gin
1½ oz. orange juice
½ oz. lemon juice
½ oz. orgeat
½ oz. sherry

Shake all but the sherry vigorously with ice and strain into a Collins glass filled with crushed ice; or blend with ¾ cup of crushed ice until smooth and pour unstrained into a Collins glass. Top with fresh crushed ice as needed. Float sherry on top. Garnish with a sprig of mint and drink through a straw.

French 75

1½ oz. London dry gin
¾ oz. simple syrup
½ oz. lemon juice
2½ oz. sparkling wine

Shake all but the wine with ice. Double strain into a chilled flute and top with sparkling wine. Garnish with a long, thin twist of lemon.

Frisco Sour

2 oz. rye whiskey
½ oz. Bénédictine
½ oz. lemon juice

Shake with ice. Strain into a chilled
cocktail glass.

*If made without lemon juice and
stirred instead of shaken, it is simply
called the Frisco; a lemon peel garnish
is appropriate in this case.*

*I*n 2010, a *New York Times* columnist named Frank Bruni fell in love with a drink without knowing what it was, then spent a month trying with increasing desperation to track it down. His was a common experience during the cocktail revival, although Bruni got his answer relatively quickly: he had friends in high places, including Audrey Saunders of Pegu Club and Jim Meehan of PDT. The mystery drink turned out to be a Frisco Sour, a classic that hadn't caught fire during the Cocktail Renaissance. So he wrote up the story and put the Gray Lady's spotlight on the recipe.

Gibson

2 oz. London dry gin
½ oz. dry vermouth

Stir with ice and strain into a chilled
cocktail glass. Garnish with a cocktail
onion.

Gimlet

2 oz. London dry gin
¾ oz. lime cordial

Shake briefly with ice and strain into
a rocks glass with ice; or, long shake
with ice and strain into a chilled
cocktail glass. Optionally, garnish
with a lime wheel.

Gin-Gin Mute

1½ oz. London dry gin
1 oz. simple syrup
¾ oz. lime juice
1 oz. ginger beer
~12 mint leaves

Shake all but the ginger beer. Strain
into a chilled highball glass and top
with ginger beer. Garnish with a sprig
of mint.

Gin and Tonic

2 oz. gin
4 oz. tonic water
wedge of lime

Combine gin and tonic water in
a highball glass with ice and stir.
Squeeze lime wedge over the glass
and drop it in.

Gin Fizz

2 oz. Old Tom gin or London dry gin
juice of ½ lemon (¾ oz.)
¼ oz. sugar
3–4 oz. seltzer

Shake all but seltzer with ice. Strain
into a highball glass without ice and top
with seltzer.

Gin Rickey

1½ oz. Old Tom gin or London dry gin
juice of ½ lime (½ oz.)
3 oz. seltzer

Juice half a lime into a highball glass.
Add ice, gin, and seltzer, and stir.
Garnish with the spent lime shell.

Gold Rush

2 oz. bourbon
¾ oz. lemon juice
½ oz. honey

Shake without ice, then again with
ice. Strain into a chilled cocktail or
rocks glass.

Grasshopper

1 oz. crème de menthe (green)
1 oz. crème de cacao (white)
1½ oz. light cream or half-and-half

Shake with ice. Strain into a chilled
cocktail glass. Optionally, garnish with
shaved chocolate.

Greyhound

1½ oz. vodka
4 oz. grapefruit juice

Combine ingredients in a highball glass
with ice and stir.

Harvey Wallbanger

1½ oz. vodka
4 oz. orange juice
½ oz. Galliano

Combine vodka and orange juice in a
highball glass with ice and stir. Float
Galliano on top.

Hemingway Daiquiri

1¾ oz. unaged or filtered
   lightly aged rum
¾ oz. maraschino liqueur
1 oz. lime juice
¾ oz. grapefruit juice
¼ oz. simple syrup

Shake with ice and strain into a chilled
cocktail glass. Garnish with a lime
wheel, a brandied cherry, or both.

While Hemingway lived in Cuba, he frequented the famous Bar La Florida (affectionately nicknamed "El Floridita"), which was owned and tended by El Rey de los Coteleros himself, Constantino Ribalaigua Vert. Ribalaigua maintained a lauded menu of Daiquiri variations and his handiwork was mentioned in Hemingway's novel *Islands in the Stream*. What is known today as the Hemingway Daiquiri was the Floridita Daiquiri #3, but the menu item Ribalaigua actually named after him—well, kind of—was the "E. Henmiway Special," which omitted the sugar. For a Papa Doble, start there and double the rum.

Highball

2 oz. bourbon
4 oz. ginger ale

Combine ingredients in a highball glass
with ice and stir.

*"Highball" is a generic term for spirits
mixed with carbonated soft drinks. If
not specified further, whiskey with club
soda or ginger ale is usually meant, but
you can substitute your favorite spirit
or soda.*

Honeymoon

1¾ oz. high-proof apple brandy
½ oz. Bénédictine
½ oz. curaçao or triple sec
½ oz. lemon juice

Shake with ice. Strain into a chilled
cocktail glass.

Many people have never had a true apple brandy, and that's a shame. Far from the auxiliary spirit it's often treated as, apple brandy is a critical player in the classic cocktail canon, and the star of the show in stalwarts like the Jack Rose and the Widow's Kiss, as well as the Honeymoon. Moreover, it's America's original homegrown spirit: Laird & Company of New Jersey holds the first distillery license issued by the U.S. government, and has been in business long enough that George Washington once asked them to send him their recipe!

Hot Toddy

4 oz. boiling water
1½ oz. whiskey
1 tsp. sugar or honey
cinnamon stick
lemon wheel

Combine all but whiskey in a heat-safe
glass or mug and stir until sugar or
honey is dissolved. Stir in whiskey.

Hurricane

1½ oz. moderately aged rum
¾ oz. fassionola
½ oz. lemon juice

Shake with ice. Strain into a rocks glass
with ice. Optionally, garnish with a lime
wheel and a maraschino cherry.

Irish Coffee

1¼ oz. Irish whiskey
3½ oz. hot coffee
½ oz. rich demerara syrup
1 oz. heavy cream

Whisk cream gently in a bowl until
bubbles dissipate. Stir coffee, whiskey,
and demerara syrup together in a heat-
safe glass or mug. Float cream on top.

Jack Rose

2 oz. apple brandy
½ oz. grenadine
½ oz. lemon juice

Shake with ice. Strain into a chilled
cocktail glass.

Japanese

2 oz. brandy
½ oz. orgeat
2 dashes Boker's Bitters or
    Angostura bitters

Shake with ice and double strain into a
chilled cocktail glass and dash bitters
on top. Express a lemon peel over the
glass and discard.

Jasmine

1½ oz. London dry gin
¾ oz. lemon juice
¼ oz. Campari
¼ oz. curaçao or triple sec

Shake with ice. Strain into a chilled
cocktail glass.

Jungle Bird

2 oz. black rum
¾ oz. Campari
½ oz. lime juice
1 tsp. rich demerara syrup
2 oz. pineapple juice

Shake with ice until foamy. Strain into a
rocks glass with ice. Optionally, garnish
with a wedge of pineapple.

The otherwise obscure Jungle Bird's unexpected use of Campari was what caught the eye of tiki historian Jeff "Beachbum" Berry. After he included it in one of his books, it became one of the most beloved and be-riffed-on drinks in the modern canon. Exhaustive research by *ThirstMag's* Kim Choong uncovered the drink's history in 2018: Jeffrey Ong Swee Teik invented it in 1973 as a welcome cocktail for the Kuala Lumpur Hilton. The Jungle Bird has since become a national symbol for Malaysian mixologists; when Ong passed away in 2019, he was lionized in the country's press as its creator.

Kir

4½ oz. white wine
¾ oz. crème de cassis

Combine ingredients in a chilled white wine glass and gently stir.

For a Kir Royale (pictured), substitute sparkling wine for the white wine and prepare in a flute.

¾ oz. London dry gin
¾ oz. lime juice
¾ oz. maraschino liqueur
¾ oz. Green Chartreuse

Shake with ice. Strain into a chilled
cocktail glass.

Lion's Tail

2 oz. bourbon
½ oz. lime juice
½ oz. allspice dram
¼ oz. rich demerara syrup
2 dashes Angostura bitters

Shake with ice. Strain into a chilled
cocktail glass.

Little Italy

2 oz. high-proof rye whiskey
¾ oz. sweet vermouth
½ oz. Cynar

Stir with ice. Strain into a chilled
cocktail glass and garnish with three
brandied or maraschino cherries on a
skewer.

Audrey Saunders is well represented in these pages. A pioneer in New York's cocktail renaissance, her exacting recipe R&D process is the stuff of legend, and has made her a prolific creator of contemporary classics, including the Old Cuban and the Gin-Gin Mule. In 2005, she opened Pegu Club (in partnership with friend and fellow pioneer Julie Reiner) and blew the doors off New York City. The Little Italy was created for the new bar, its ingredients and name an homage to the neighborhood, and to the growing cocktail revival.

Long Island Iced Tea

½ oz. gin
½ oz. blanco tequila
½ oz. lightly aged rum
½ oz. vodka
½ oz. curaçao or triple sec
½ oz. lemon juice
½ oz. simple syrup
3 oz. cola

Combine ingredients in a Collins glass
with ice and stir. Garnish with a wedge
or slice of lemon.

Madras

1½ oz. vodka
3 oz. cranberry juice cocktail
1 oz. orange juice
wedge of lime

Combine vodka, cranberry juice cocktail, and orange juice in a highball glass with ice and stir. Squeeze lime wedge over the glass and drop it in.

One of several similar variations on the Cape Codder. For a Sea Breeze, substitute 1 oz. of grapefruit juice for the orange juice. For a Bay Breeze, substitute 1 oz. of pineapple juice for the orange juice.

Mai Tai

2 oz. aged rum · ¾ oz. lime juice
½ oz. curaçao or triple sec
½ oz. orgeat

Shake with crushed ice, or long shake
with cubed ice. Pour unstrained into a
rocks glass, or double strain into a rocks
glass filled with crushed ice. Garnish with
a spent lime shell and a sprig of mint.

*The best Mai Tais are usually made
with a house rum blend, which you can
approximate using, for example, 1 oz. each
of two different rums. Personally, I enjoy
combining a Jamaican black rum with a
long-aged Barbados rum.*

Manhattan

2 oz. rye whiskey
1 oz. sweet vermouth
2 dashes Angostura bitters

Stir with ice. Strain into a chilled cocktail glass and garnish with a brandied or maraschino cherry.

The origins of the most classic cocktails are invariably lost to time. This can be a function of their simplicity: a drink with three common ingredients was probably invented multiple times before it was written down. But it has never stopped anyone from *claiming* to know the history. The Manhattan is often said to have been invented by Winston Churchill's mother at a party for Samuel Tilden's gubernatorial inauguration, even though she was in Britain with a one-month-old future prime minister at the time. Most likely, it came out of the Manhattan Club in New York sometime in the 1870s.

Margarita

2 oz. blanco or reposado tequila
½ oz. curaçao or triple sec
½ oz. lime juice
1 tsp. simple syrup

Shake with ice. Strain into a chilled cocktail glass with a salted rim. Garnish with a lime wheel or a lime wedge.

For a Tommy's Margarita, leave out the simple syrup and the curaçao or triple sec, and add ½ oz. agave nectar.

Martinez

2 oz. sweet vermouth
1 oz. Old Tom gin
1 tsp. maraschino liqueur
2 dashes Boker's Bitters or
  Angostura bitters

Stir with ice and strain into a chilled
cocktail glass.

*S*ome sources claim the Martinez as the ancestor of the Martini, but this is unlikely. According to David Wondrich, there were equivalent recipes circulating in the late nineteenth century for the Martine, Martineau, Martina, Martena, Martigny, Martini, and Martinez, each of them calling for sweet vermouth (the dry stuff would come later) and Old Tom gin (ditto). From this soup evolved the Martini we know and love, while "Martinez" has stuck as the modern name for any recipe along the lines of those early Martin[x] concoctions. This one dates to 1887 and comes via Wondrich's book *Imbibe!*

Martini

3 oz. London dry gin
1 oz. dry vermouth
1 dash orange bitters (optional)

Stir with ice. Strain into a chilled
cocktail glass and garnish with an olive
or a lemon twist.

Maximilian Affair

1 oz. mezcal
1 oz. elderflower liqueur
½ oz. Punt e Mes
½ oz. lemon juice

Shake with ice. Strain into a chilled cocktail glass.

The Maximilian Affair showcases three ingredients that first gained popularity during the cocktail revival: mezcal, Punt e Mes, and elderflower liqueur, which got so common it was nicknamed "bartender's ketchup." The drink rose to prominence after its inventor, Misty Kalkofen, used it in a St. Germain recipe competition. It appeared in *Food & Wine*'s 2009 cocktail guide, and was adapted by Eric Felten for the *Wall Street Journal*. It remains a handshake drink in Boston, often abbreviated to the "Max. Affair" when ordered. Appropriately, Misty eventually left bartending to sell mezcal, and coauthored a book called *Drinking Like Ladies*, which highlights contemporary recipes by women in hospitality.

Mimosa

3 oz. chilled orange juice
3 oz. chilled sparkling wine

Pour orange juice into a chilled flute, followed by sparkling wine. Stir gently to combine.

For a Buck's Fizz, use 2 oz. orange juice and 4 oz. sparkling wine instead.

Mint Julep

2 oz. bourbon
½ oz. simple syrup
3–4 sprigs of mint

Shake bourbon and simple syrup with ice. Strain into a silver Julep cup filled with crushed ice. Insert a straw and surround it with the sprigs of mint, so that they must be smelled while drinking.

There's no need to muddle your mint or make it into a syrup. For the mintiest Mint Julep you've ever had, get a big bunch of mint, smack it against the back of your hand to release the oils, and arrange it in the glass so you have to smell it as you drink. You'll never notice that there's no mint actually *in* the drink. Flavor incorporates both taste and smell, and because we can distinguish only a small number of tastes (sweet, sour, salty, bitter, and savory) but tens of thousands of distinct scent chemicals, flavor perception is heavily weighted towards smell.

Mojito

1½ oz. unaged or filtered lightly
   aged rum
juice of ½ lime
½ oz. simple syrup
2 oz. seltzer
~12 mint leaves

Shake all but seltzer. Strain into a
highball glass and top with seltzer.
Garnish with a sprig of mint.

Moscow Mule

1½ oz. vodka
4 oz. ginger beer
wedge of lime

Combine vodka and ginger beer in a
highball glass or copper mug and stir.
Squeeze lime wedge over the glass and
drop it in.

Navy Grog

1 oz. filtered lightly aged rum
1 oz. Jamaican black rum
1 oz. overproof black rum
¾ oz. lime juice
¾ oz. grapefruit juice
¾ oz. seltzer
½ oz. honey

Shake without ice, then shake vigorously
with ice. Pour unstrained into a rocks glass,
or strain into a rocks glass with an ice cone.
(To make an ice cone, fill a pilsner glass
with shaved ice, insert a chopstick or metal
straw to make a hole in the middle, and
freeze until solid. Feed a straw through the
hole and serve large-side down.)

The man who created "tiki" as a cultural and mixological phenomenon went by the name "Don the Beachcomber." (He was born Earnest Raymond Beaumont Gantt, but had it legally changed to Donn Beach.) His first student, Victor Jules Bergeron ("Trader Vic" to his friends), would also become his biggest rival. As they built nationwide commercial empires they fought frequently over who had stolen what from whom. Donn came up with his Navy Grog first, and I think his is the better drink. For Vic's version, cut the honey and seltzer and add ¼ oz. allspice dram and ½ oz. rich demerara syrup.

Negroni

1 oz. London dry gin
1 oz. Campari
1 oz. sweet vermouth

Combine ingredients in a rocks glass
with ice and stir. Garnish with an
orange peel.

*For a Negroni Sbagliato, replace the gin
with 2 oz. of sparkling wine.*

New York Flip

1¼ oz. bourbon
1 oz. tawny port
1 tsp. rich demerara syrup
whole egg

Shake without ice, then again with ice. Strain into a chilled cocktail glass and garnish with a sprinkle of grated nutmeg.

New York Sour

2 oz. high-proof rye whiskey
1 oz. simple syrup
¾ oz. lemon juice
½ oz. dry red wine

Shake all but the wine with ice. Strain into a rocks glass with ice and float wine on top.

Nightglow

2 oz. brandy
½ oz. kirschwasser
½ oz. simple syrup
¼ oz. lemon juice
2 dashes Peychaud's Bitters

Shake with ice. Strain into a chilled
cocktail glass.

Oaxaca Old Fashioned

1½ oz. reposado tequila
½ oz. mezcal
1 tsp. agave nectar
2 dashes Angostura bitters

Combine ingredients in a rocks glass
with ice and stir. Flame an orange peel
over the glass and drop it in.

Old Cuban

1½ oz. moderately aged rum
1 oz. simple syrup
¾ oz. lime juice
6 mint leaves
2 dashes Angostura bitters
2 oz. sparkling wine

Shake all but the wine with ice. Strain
into a chilled cocktail glass and top with
sparkling wine.

Old Fashioned

2 oz. bourbon or rye whiskey
2 tsp. sugar
3 dashes Angostura bitters
splash of water

In a rocks glass, muddle sugar with
water and bitters until dissolved. Add
ice and whiskey, and stir. Express an
orange peel over the glass and drop it in.

Palmetto

1½ oz. aged rum
1 oz. sweet vermouth
2 dashes orange bitters

Stir with ice. Strain into a chilled
cocktail glass.

Paloma

2 oz. blanco or reposado tequila
½ oz. lime juice
1 pinch salt
4 oz. grapefruit soda

Combine ingredients in a highball glass
with ice and stir.

The *changuirongo*, a tequila highball made with any sort of soda,
has been known in Mexico since at
least the 1940s. But although Squirt
began selling a grapefruit soda there
in 1955, their story dating the Paloma
to the '50s seems to be a marketing
myth. Camper English of *Alcademics*
has researched the drink's history
extensively, finding references to a
tequila-Squirt-grapefruit juice drink
going back to the '80s but no "Paloma"
until the final years of the century.
Whatever the drink's history, tequila
and grapefruit make a delicious combination, rightly popular on both sides
of the Rio Grande.

Paper Plane

¾ oz. bourbon
¾ oz. Aperol
¾ oz. Amaro Nonino
¾ oz. lemon juice

Shake with ice. Strain into a chilled
cocktail glass.

Pegu Club

1½ oz. London dry gin
¾ oz. curaçao or triple sec
¾ oz. lime juice
1 dash Angostura bitters
1 dash orange bitters

Shake with ice and strain into a chilled
cocktail glass. Optionally, garnish with
a lime peel.

Pendennis Club

2 oz. London dry gin
1 oz. apricot liqueur
¾ oz. lime juice
3 dashes Peychaud's Bitters

Shake with ice. Strain into a chilled cocktail glass.

Penicillin

2 oz. blended Scotch
¾ oz. lemon juice
⅓ oz. ginger syrup
⅓ oz. honey
¼ oz. smoky Islay Scotch

Shake all but the Islay Scotch without
ice, then again with ice. Strain into a
rocks glass with ice. Float Islay Scotch
on top and garnish with a piece of
candied ginger.

*P*erhaps the most famous contemporary classic cocktail, the Penicillin is at any rate the biggest name to emerge from the late Sasha Petraske's lower Manhattan bar, Milk and Honey, which inspired a thousand neo-speakeasies around the world. The Penicillin was bartender Sam Ross's brainchild but hewed to the Petraskean principle of controlled innovation grounded in mastery of the classics. The result is an elaboration on the Gold Rush, which in turn is an adaptation of the Bec's Knees, another Milk and Honey favorite. Naturally, it has become a popular base for further riffing, including the dry shake version seen here.

Pimm's Cup

2 oz. Pimm's No. 1 Cup
½ oz. lemon juice
3–4 slices cucumber
4 oz. ginger ale or lemon soda

In a highball glass, stack ice cubes and
cucumber slices in alternating layers.
Stir Pimm's and lemon juice without ice
and pour over stack. Fill with ginger ale
or lemon soda. Garnish with seasonal
berries, mint, and/or more cucumber,
as desired.

Piña Colada

1 oz. coconut cream
3 oz. pineapple juice
2½ oz. lightly aged rum

Combine ingredients in a blender with
¾ cup of crushed ice and blend for 5–10
seconds. Pour unstrained into a Collins
glass or the decorative vessel of your
choice and drink through a straw.

Pink Lady

1½ oz. London dry gin
½ oz. apple brandy
¾ oz. lemon juice
½ oz. simple syrup
½ oz. grenadine
egg white

Shake without ice, then again with ice.
Strain into a chilled cocktail glass.

People are often wary of raw-egg drinks like the Pink Lady, but you don't have to be. If you've had poached, soft-boiled, over easy, or sunny-side up eggs, you've already eaten eggs that were "undercooked" according to CDC guidelines, and chances are you didn't get sick. In fact, it's relatively hard to get *Salmonella* from eggs these days: The bacteria live on the outside of the shell, not the inside, and eggs have to undergo a sterilizing wash before they reach U.S. grocery stores. So be fearless, and enjoy the foamy texture of a classic egg cocktail!

Pisco Sour

1½ oz. Pisco
½ oz. simple syrup
½ oz. lemon juice
egg white

Shake without ice, then again with ice. Strain into a chilled cocktail glass. Optionally, decorate with 1–5 drops of Amargo Chuncho or Angostura bitters.

Sometimes called the "Peruvian-style" Pisco Sour, the Chilean style lacking the egg white and bitters.

Planter's Punch

1 of sour · 2 of sweet
3 of strong · 4 of weak

And a bit of spice to make it nice.

"Planter's Punch" isn't a drink but a kind of drink, based on rum and these traditional rhyming proportions. No two printed recipes are alike. You can make your own at home, with your choice of citrus fruit(s) for the sour; of sugar, syrups, or liqueurs for the sweet; and of rum(s) for the strong. Ice, particularly crushed ice, should satisfy the weak. Bitters will work for the spice, but you can also try a spicy liqueur like allspice dram.

*I*t has been observed that the entire genre of tiki drinks exists within the Planter's Punch. The "rum rhapsodies" Donn Beach created are all elaborations on what David Embury called the Sour type of cocktail, drinks principally defined by the addition of citrus and sweeteners, rather than being driven by vermouth or other primarily bitter aromatizing elements. The Beachcomber's great innovation was introducing variety within his ingredient categories. Why not split the sour between two citrus juices, or the sweetener between three syrups? There's a reason his most-quoted maxim is, "What one rum can't do, three rums can."

Ramos Gin Fizz

2 oz. London dry gin
¾ oz. simple syrup
¾ oz. heavy cream
½ oz. lemon juice
½ oz. lime juice
3 drops orange flower water
egg white
1½ oz. seltzer

Pour seltzer into a chilled Collins glass.
Shake remaining ingredients without
ice for a full minute. (When it feels like
there's a piece of rope bouncing back and
forth in the shaker, you've shaken it long
enough.) Shake again (briefly) with ice,
and strain into the Collins glass.

Red Hook

2 oz. rye whiskey
½ oz. maraschino liqueur
½ oz. Punt e Mes

Stir with ice. Strain into a chilled
cocktail glass.

Remember the Maine

2 oz. high-proof rye whiskey
¾ oz. sweet vermouth
½ oz. Cherry Heering
½ tsp. absinthe

Stir with ice and strain into a chilled
cocktail glass. Optionally, express a
lemon peel over the glass.

Rob Roy

2 oz. blended Scotch
1 oz. sweet vermouth
2 dashes Angostura bitters

Stir with ice and strain into a chilled
cocktail glass. Express an orange peel
over the glass and discard.

Rose

2 oz. dry vermouth
1 oz. kirschwasser
1 tsp. raspberry syrup

Stir with ice and strain into a chilled cocktail glass. Optionally, garnish with a brandied or maraschino cherry.

Rosita

1½ oz. reposado tequila
½ oz. Campari
½ oz. sweet vermouth
½ oz. dry vermouth
2 dashes Angostura bitters

Stir with ice and strain into a chilled cocktail glass. Express a lemon peel over the glass and discard.

Rusty Nail

1½ oz. blended Scotch
½ oz. Drambuie

Combine ingredients in a rocks glass
with ice and stir.

*For a Godfather, substitute ¾ oz. of
amaretto for the Drambuie.*

Saturn

1½ oz. London dry gin
½ oz. lemon juice
½ oz. orgeat
¼ oz. passion fruit syrup
¼ oz. falernum

Shake vigorously with ice and strain
into a rocks glass filled with crushed
ice; or blend with ½ cup of crushed ice
until smooth and pour unstrained into
a rocks glass. Top with fresh crushed
ice as needed. Garnish with a long, thin
twist of lime wrapped around a cherry
on a skewer.

Tiki garnishes are known for being elaborate, but they're often symbolic, too! The Mai Tai is traditionally garnished with a lime shell and a mint sprig, like there's a little tropical island with a palm tree atop the drink. The World War II–era Three Dots and a Dash uses three cherries and a pineapple cube to represent its namesake Morse Code transmission (a "*V*" for victory). The Saturn's decoration is meant to look like a ringed planet—be sure to leave space between the cherry and the lime peel for the full effect!

Sazerac

2 oz. rye whiskey
1 tsp. simple syrup
4 dashes Peychaud's Bitters
1 dash Angostura bitters
1 tsp. absinthe (rinse)

Combine all but absinthe in a rocks glass and stir with ice. Strain into a second, chilled rocks glass rinsed with absinthe. Express a lemon peel over the glass and discard.

Scofflaw

1½ oz. rye whiskey
1 oz. dry vermouth
¾ oz. lemon juice
½ oz. grenadine
1 dash orange bitters

Shake with ice and strain into a chilled
cocktail glass and dash bitters on top.
Optionally, garnish with an orange peel.

In 1924, Delcevare King of Quincy, Massachusetts, sponsored a newspaper contest with a $200 prize, seeking a new word to describe his countrymen who were flouting the Volstead Act. (King was a leader of the local Anti-Saloon League.) He stipulated that the word had to begin with "*S*"—it had a sting, he said—and two people submitted "scofflaw," which won. A new word had entered the English language in support of Prohibition. A Scofflaw cocktail was promptly invented for the ex-pat crowd at Harry's New York Bar in Paris.

Scorpion

2 oz. lightly aged rum
2 oz. London dry gin
2 oz. orange juice · 1½ oz. brandy
⅔ oz. orgeat · ½ oz. lime juice
½ oz. rich demerara syrup

Combine in a blender with 1 cup of crushed ice and blend for 5–10 seconds. Pour unstrained into a Scorpion bowl or other communal vessel and drink with long straws. Serves 2–3 people.

Can be halved for a single-serve drink as depicted, or multiplied to fit the size of your party (and your Scorpion Bowl).

Screwdriver

1½ oz. vodka
4 oz. orange juice

Combine ingredients in a highball glass
with ice and stir.

*For a Garibaldi, substitute 1½ oz. of
Campari for the vodka.*

Seelbach

1 oz. bourbon
½ oz. curaçao or triple sec
7 dashes Angostura bitters
7 dashes Peychaud's Bitters
3–4 oz. sparkling wine

Stir all but the wine with ice. Strain into a chilled flute and fill with sparkling wine. Garnish with an orange twist.

Sherry Cobbler

4 oz. sherry
½ oz. sugar
3 orange slices

Shake with ice. Pour unstrained into a
highball glass, or strain into a highball
glass filled with crushed ice. Garnish
with seasonal berries, a sprig of mint,
and/or more slices of orange or lemon,
as desired, and drink through a straw.

Shirley Temple

6 oz. ginger ale
½ oz. grenadine

Pour ginger ale into a highball glass full of ice. Drizzle in grenadine. Garnish with several maraschino cherries (the bright red, nonalcoholic kind).

For a Roy Rogers, substitute cola for the ginger ale.

Sidecar

2 oz. brandy
¾ oz. curaçao or triple sec
¾ oz. lemon juice
1 tsp. rich demerara syrup (optional)

Shake with ice and strain into a chilled cocktail glass. If not using demerara syrup, sugar the rim of the glass first.

Siesta

1½ oz. blanco tequila
¾ oz. simple syrup
½ oz. lime juice
½ oz. grapefruit juice
¼ oz. Campari

Shake with ice. Strain into a chilled
cocktail glass.

Silver Fizz

2 oz. Old Tom gin or London dry gin
juice of ½ lemon (¾ oz.)
¼ oz. sugar
egg white
3 oz. seltzer

Shake all but seltzer without ice, then
again with ice. Strain into a highball
glass without ice and top with seltzer.

*For a Golden Fizz, use the yolk of the egg
instead of the white.*

Singapore Sling

1½ London dry gin
¾ oz. Cherry Heering
¼ oz. Bénédictine
¼ oz. curaçao or triple sec
½ oz. lime juice
¼ oz. grenadine
1 dash Angostura bitters
2 oz. pineapple juice
½ oz. seltzer

Pour seltzer into the bottom of a Collins
glass. Shake remaining ingredients with ice
until foamy, then strain into glass and add
ice to fill. Garnish with a cherry and a slice
of pineapple.

Tiki is a Californian phenomenon, combining Caribbean drink templates with the aesthetics of an imagined Polynesia for the escapist needs of the 1930s. Unique among its standard canon, the Singapore Sling is the genuine article, invented in its namesake city long before Donn Beach and Trader Vic were running bars. It is usually attributed to Raffles Hotel barman Ngiam Tong Boon, although the details of its creation are hazy. Sadly, it still suffered the common tiki fate of morphing into vaguely red-flavored mush in the late twentieth century. This recipe shows how it got so popular in Singapore.

Southside

2 oz. London dry gin
¾ oz. lemon juice
¾ oz. simple syrup
~8 mint leaves
1 dash orange bitters

Shake with ice and strain into a chilled
cocktail glass and dash bitters on top.
Garnish with a sprig of mint.

*For the Southside Fizz, strain into a
highball glass instead and top with
2–3 oz. of seltzer.*

Spritz

3 oz. sparkling wine
2 oz. Aperol
1 oz. seltzer

Combine ingredients in a rocks glass
with ice and stir. Garnish with a large
wedge of orange.

*Alternatively, substitute Campari or the
bitter of your choice for the Aperol.*

Stinger

1½ oz. brandy
¼ oz. crème de menthe (white)

Stir with ice and strain into a chilled
cocktail glass. Express a lemon peel
over the glass and discard.

Suffering Bastard

1 oz. London dry gin
1 oz. brandy
½ oz. lime cordial
2 dashes Angostura bitters
4 oz. ginger beer

Shake all but the ginger beer. Pour unstrained into a highball glass and fill with ginger beer. Garnish with a sprig of mint and an orange slice.

The most famous cocktail invented in Africa, the Suffering Bastard hails from the tony Shepheard's Hotel in Cairo, where in 1942 Joe Scialom served it to Allied soldiers feeling thirsty, hungover, or just sober. It's sometimes said that the name was corrupted from "Suffering Bar Steward," but that was a later bowdlerization. Later, while working for Hilton, Scialom added the Dying Bastard and the Dead Bastard to his repertoire, respectively marked by the addition of bourbon and the further addition of rum. Jeff "Beachbum" Berry worked out the recipe's history with the help of Scialom's daughter and his surviving papers.

Tequila Sunrise

1½ oz. blanco tequila
3 oz. orange juice
¾ oz. grenadine

Combine tequila and orange juice in
a highball glass with ice and stir, then
drizzle in grenadine.

*As the grenadine sinks to the bottom, it
will create the color gradient effect that
gives the cocktail its name.*

Three Dots and a Dash

1½ oz. aged Martinique rhum agricole
   or cachaça
½ oz. moderately aged rum
¼ oz. allspice dram · ¼ oz. falernum
½ oz. lime juice · ½ oz. orange juice
⅓ oz. honey · 1 dash Angostura bitters

Shake vigorously with ice and strain
into a rocks glass filled with crushed
ice. Garnish with three cherries and a
chunk of pineapple on a skewer.

Ti' Punch

2 oz. unaged Martinique
   rhum agricole
1 tsp. cane syrup

Combine ingredients in a rocks glass
without ice and swizzle. Cut a quarter-
sized round from the side of a lime,
including some of the flesh; squeeze
6–10 drops of lime juice into the drink
to taste and drop the lime round in.

*For a Ti' Punch Vieux, substitute an aged
Martinique rhum agricole.*

The national drink of Martinique, the Ti' Punch highlights the surprisingly savory and vegetal character of the island's rhums agricoles, and the wonderful grassiness of sugarcane syrup. Martin Cate writes in *Smuggler's Cove* that on Martinique you're usually served the components separately and combine them to your taste, a custom known as "chacun prépare sa propre mort," or "each prepares his own death." (They even give you a full bottle of rum, though without enough lime to finish it.) Its popularity in the U.S. owes a lot to importer Ed Hamilton. Add ice if you like, but it's better without.

Tom Collins

2 oz. Old Tom gin
juice of ½ lemon (¾ oz.)
1 tsp. sugar
6 oz. seltzer

Combine gin, lemon, and sugar
in a Collins glass with ice and stir.
Fill with seltzer.

1 oz. aquavit
1 oz. sherry
1 oz. Cynar
2 dashes peach bitters

Combine ingredients in a rocks glass
with ice and stir.

Trinidad Sour

1 oz. Angostura bitters
1 oz. orgeat
½ oz. high-proof rye whiskey
¾ oz. lemon juice

Shake with ice. Strain into a chilled
cocktail glass.

Twelve-Mile Limit

1 oz. lightly aged rum
½ oz. brandy
½ oz. rye whiskey
½ oz. grenadine
½ oz. lemon juice

Shake with ice and strain into a chilled cocktail glass. Garnish with a brandied or maraschino cherry.

Twentieth Century

1½ oz. London dry gin
¾ oz. Kina apéritif wine
½ oz. crème de cacao (white)
½ oz. lemon juice

Shake with ice and strain into a chilled
cocktail glass. Optionally, garnish with
a lemon peel.

Vermouth Cocktail

1 oz. sweet vermouth
1 oz. dry vermouth
1 dash orange bitters

Stir with ice. Strain into a chilled
cocktail glass. Optionally, garnish with a
brandied or maraschino cherry.

*It is also common to substitute another
type of bitters or to use either sweet or
dry vermouth exclusively.*

Vesper

3 oz. London dry gin
1 oz. vodka
½ oz. Kina apéritif wine

Shake with ice. Strain into a chilled
cocktail glass and garnish with a long,
thin twist of lemon.

*I*nvented by Ian Fleming, this is the drink that first made "shaken, not stirred" a James Bond catchphrase. In *Casino Royale*, the drink is 007's own creation and named after his love interest Vesper Lynd. Ironically, Fleming didn't try it until after the book was published—and he didn't care for it when he did!

In general, shaking will dilute a drink more than stirring will. The Vesper, with its heavy pour of spirits and scant share of wine, can stand a little watering down; but if you're mixing a Martini, you're better off stirring.

Vieux Carré

1 oz. rye whiskey
1 oz. brandy
1 oz. sweet vermouth
1 tsp. Bénédictine
2 dashes Angostura bitters
2 dashes Peychaud's Bitters

Stir with ice. Strain into a chilled rocks glass. Optionally, garnish with a lemon peel.

Vodka Espresso

1½ oz. vodka
1 oz. espresso
¾ oz. coffee liqueur

Shake with ice until foamy. Strain into
a chilled cocktail glass and garnish with
three coffee beans.

Vodka Sour

1½ oz. vodka
1 oz. simple syrup
¾ oz. lemon juice

Shake with ice. Strain into a chilled
cocktail glass.

*For a Lemon Drop, add ½ oz. of curaçao
or triple sec and reduce the lemon juice
and simple syrup to ½ oz. each.*

Ward Eight

1¾ oz. high-proof rye whiskey
¾ oz. grenadine
½ oz. lemon juice
¼ oz. orange juice

Shake with ice and strain into a chilled
cocktail glass. Optionally, garnish with
a brandied or maraschino cherry.

The Ward Eight's history is full of both credulous and revisionist falsehoods. The drink was definitely invented in Boston, probably in 1898 at Locke-Ober. Some say it was created on election night for ward boss Martin Lomasney, but he wasn't there, didn't drink, and lost badly that year. Others say that Lomasney was a prohibitionist (he wasn't), that grenadine wasn't in the U.S. yet (it was, since 1872) and wasn't being used in cocktails (it was in France, and Locke-Ober was a French restaurant). Brother Cleve, Boston's cocktail godfather, says this recipe from Chad Arnholt is the best he's had.

Water Lily

¾ oz. London dry gin
¾ oz. curaçao or triple sec
¾ oz. crème de violette
¾ oz. lemon juice

Shake with ice. Strain into a chilled
cocktail glass.

Whiskey Sour

2 oz. bourbon
1 oz. simple syrup
¾ oz. lemon juice

Shake with ice. Strain into a chilled
cocktail glass.

*For a Boston Sour, add an egg white and
shake without ice then again with ice.*

White Lady

2 oz. London dry gin
½ oz. curaçao or triple sec
½ oz. lemon juice
egg white

Shake without ice, then again with ice.
Strain into a chilled cocktail glass.

Prohibition drove American drinkers across the ocean, and two men called Harry awaited them in Europe. Harry MacElhone ran Harry's New York Bar in Paris, Harry Craddock the American Bar at London's Savoy Hotel. Each of them had a White Lady recipe, with Craddock's being the closer to our modern version, but the egg white would not be added until the 1940s. It has since become the standard. Don't worry, each Harry still has a secure legacy: MacElhone published several influential cocktail guides, and Craddock wrote London's backbar bible, the *Savoy Cocktail Book*. Both of their bars remain open to this day.

White Russian

2 oz. coffee liqueur
1 oz. vodka
2 oz. light cream or half-and-half

Combine ingredients in a rocks
glass with ice and stir; or, roll between
two tins with ice and strain into a
chilled cocktail glass.

Widow's Kiss

1½ oz. apple brandy
¾ oz. Bénédictine
¾ oz. Yellow Chartreuse
2 dashes Angostura bitters

Stir with ice. Strain into a chilled
cocktail glass.

Yale Cocktail

2 oz. London dry gin
⅓ oz. dry vermouth
⅓ oz. crème de violette
1 dash Angostura bitters

Stir with ice. Strain into a chilled
cocktail glass.

Yellow Jacket

2 oz. reposado tequila
1 oz. elderflower liqueur
¾ oz. Yellow Chartreuse
1 dash orange bitters

Stir with ice and strain into a chilled
cocktail glass. Express a lemon peel
over the glass and discard.

The Yellow Jacket was invented at New York neo-speakeasy Employees Only, its creation made possible by the revival of orange bitters, in particular the ones made by Sazerac in partnership with the late Gary "gaz" Regan. As an author and educator, gaz was a forerunner of the Cocktail Renaissance and a mentor to a generation of bartenders. His namesake bitters are adapted from a recipe in Charles H. Baker's *The Gentleman's Companion*. An earlier draft was so tasty that the Alcohol Tax and Trade Bureau refused to approve its sale as a bitters, apparently believing people would drink it straight.

Zombie

1½ oz. moderately aged Puerto Rican rum
1½ oz. Jamaican black rum
1 oz. overproof black rum
¾ oz. lime juice · ½ oz. falernum
⅓ oz. grapefruit juice
1 tsp. cinnamon simple syrup
1 tsp. grenadine · 6 drops pastis
1 dash Angostura bitters

Shake vigorously with ice and strain into
a Zombie or Collins glass filled with ¾ cup
of crushed ice; or blend with crushed ice
for five seconds and pour unstrained into a
Zombie glass. Top with fresh crushed ice as
needed. Garnish with a sprig of mint.

Ingredients and Substitutions

You may not have everything in this book in your pantry already. That's OK! What follows is some information on stocking up, substituting, and cooking your way to as full a pantry and bar as you desire.

Bitters

Six types are mentioned in this book. The first two are required, the third is strongly recommended, and the others are there in case you get really interested in bitters.

Angostura Bitters: A rich, spicy bitters from Trinidad, and by far the most common cocktail bitters. Available in most grocery stores. Products from other brands labeled "aromatic bitters" may be viable substitutes.

Orange Bitters: A category, not a brand, describing any cocktail bitters primarily flavored with oranges. Regan's No. 6 is a good choice, but most bitters companies make an orange bitters now.

Peychaud's Bitters: The traditional New Orleans bitters, with notes of anise and stone fruit. Products from other brands labeled "creole bitters" or something similar may be viable substitutes.

Boker's Bitters: A major bitters brand during the nineteenth century. Long defunct. Generally understood to have been a woodsy aromatic bitters with notes of cardamom and coffee. Several modern reconstructions exist under this name or "Bogart's Bitters." Angostura is an acceptable alternative in all the Boker's recipes in this book.

Amargo Chuncho: A Peruvian bitters made with local ingredients. The best option for decorating a Pisco Sour, and worth trying in recipes that call for Angostura or Boker's.

Peach Bitters: Like orange bitters, this is a category, but the most common type is from Fee Bros. A great way to liven up highballs and other long drinks.

Syrups

I've ordered these by their importance, in my view, and the ease of preparing them at home. The first three, in particular, require so little effort and are so useful that there's no good reason not to make them yourself. That said, it should be noted that bottled versions of all of these are available for purchase.

If making syrup at home, I recommend clear plastic squeeze bottles (like those used for condiments or cake decorating) for easiest storage and use. In my personal experience, all of these can keep for many weeks without issue, but use good judgment: if it smells funny or things start floating in it, throw it out. Then make a new batch and make more cocktails to go through it faster.

Simple Syrup: Combine equal parts of white sugar and water in a container. Shake briefly until sugar is dissolved. Refrigerate. That's it!

Grenadine: Combine equal parts of pomegranate juice and white sugar in a container. Shake briefly until sugar is dissolved. Refrigerate. Alternatively, combine ingredients in a pot, stir to combine, and gradually reduce the mixture until it reaches your desired viscosity. Some recipes also add orange flower water, fresh citrus juice, or a bit of liquor as a preservative.

Rich Demerara Syrup: Combine two parts demerara sugar and one part water in a small pot. Warm the mixture and stir until dissolved, then bottle and refrigerate.

Note that you can also make a rich simple syrup in this way, or a 1:1 demerara syrup using the simple syrup instructions above. I find that cocktails that benefit from the richer texture of 2:1 simple syrup also benefit from the richer flavor of demerara sugar, which is why I classify them separately.

Raspberry Syrup: Take one part fresh or frozen raspberries and mash them. Add two parts white sugar and mix well. Allow to macerate for 30 minutes. Add one part warm (not hot or boiling) water and stir until sugar is dissolved. Pour through a fine mesh strainer to remove the seeds. Bottle and refrigerate.

Note that grenadine and raspberry syrup can often be substituted for one another in cocktails. The recipes in this book reflect standard practice, and it's the standard for a reason, but feel free to experiment.

Ginger Syrup: Peel and finely chop one part fresh ginger root. Combine in a small pot with one part sugar and two parts water. Bring the mixture to a boil and stir to dissolve sugar. Reduce heat and simmer until flavor is well extracted (that could be as little as 10 minutes for a small batch, but probably at least 20–30 minutes if you're using a full cup of ginger). Strain to remove the now-candied ginger pieces, bottle, and refrigerate. Be sure to save those candied ginger pieces for cooking!

To make homemade ginger beer, mix one part ginger syrup with three parts seltzer. For ginger ale, mix one part ginger syrup with one part simple syrup and six parts seltzer.

Cinnamon Simple Syrup: Combine equal parts sugar and water in a small pot, with 3–4 cinnamon sticks per cup of water. Bring to a boil and stir until sugar dissolves. Reduce heat and simmer for a few minutes (no less than two, no more than ten, depending on desired concentration). Then remove from heat and allow to stand until desired strength of cinnamon flavor is achieved. Remove cinnamon, straining out any broken-off pieces if necessary, then bottle and refrigerate. If you prefer to buy a bottled syrup, BG Reynolds makes a nice one.

Honey Syrup: Many bartenders find honey too viscous for convenient bar use and prefer to make a honey syrup instead. I disagree, and throughout this book I instead recommend dry shaking honey to integrate it better (as we do for egg whites). There are also less-viscous varieties of honey that are easier to pour, like Atchafalaya honey from Louisiana. If, however, you'd prefer to make a honey syrup, you may do so by combining three parts honey with one part warm water and stirring until well combined. Dry shaking is unnecessary with a honey syrup, but may still help build up an aromatic foam. Note however that when using a honey syrup in place of honey, you should increase the volume; I find that ¾ oz. of syrup is roughly equivalent to ½ oz. of plain honey.

Lime Cordial: It is possible to make lime cordial at home, but it is much easier to get a bottled product. BG Reynolds and El Guapo are the best I've had; avoid Rose's, which I have to think is a shadow of its former self. If you'd like to try to make it at home, this is the easiest way: Peel some number of limes. Put the peels in a bowl and add between ¾ oz. and 1 oz. of white sugar for each lime. Mix very well and let sit for at least half an hour; the sugar should draw the lime oils out of the peels and the mixture should become wet. When ready, juice the peeled limes and strain the pulp out of the juice. Stir the juice into the bowl until the sugar is dissolved. Then strain out the peels, bottle, and refrigerate. Some recipes further recommend reducing the mixture in a pot, adding lime leaves, etc.

Orgeat: Making orgeat is a lengthy process that involves a lot of soaking and grinding almonds. You're welcome to try it, but I never have. I recommend buying a bottled version. Reputable products from BG Reynolds, Latitude 29, Liber & Co., and Small Hand Foods are all available online; an expertly crafted orgeat works wonders in cocktails.

Substitutions

Some additional ways to make your life easier and/or tailor this book to what you normally have in your house:

Absinthe: If you're having trouble sourcing absinthe, you can always do what everyone did while it was banned: use pastis or the Louisiana substitute Herbsaint instead. Some producers also have wormwood or absinthe bitters, which can replace the absinthe in cocktails that call for a rinse.

Black Rum: If all you have is an unsweetened, decent quality lightly or moderately aged rum, but you want to make a black rum recipe like the Jungle Bird, you can approximate the flavor and viscosity by adding a drizzle of molasses to the drink. Failing that, double down on rich demerara syrup or one of its substitutes. It won't be quite the same, but it'll be closer.

Cachaça, cane juice rum, rhum agricole: Any of these can work in a recipe calling for any of the others, so long as it is aged (or not) to the extent the recipe calls for (with the exception of national drinks, e.g., Martinique's Ti' Punch).

Campari: Lots of Campari clones have sprung up in recent years, creating the odd category of "red bitter" or "Italian red bitter." Major houses including Luxardo, Carpano, and Martini & Rossi now have their own, as do small craft distillers across the U.S. While Campari remains the gold—er, red—standard, it's safe to say that any other brilliantly red bitter liqueur with an ABV in the 20%–30% range was designed to compete with Campari and to hold up if used in its place in cocktails. Similar products that are lower in proof may be designed to compete with **Aperol** instead, particularly if the name includes "aperitivo" or something similar.

Citrus Juice: Although one shouldn't get in the habit of it, lemon and lime juice can often be substituted for one another in cocktails without doing too much harm. Orange and grapefruit juice normally cannot. Avoid bottled lemon and lime juice entirely. Packaged orange and grapefruit juice is usually all right (ditto for pineapple juice, incidentally), although fresh-squeezed juice will still taste better. Whatever you do, avoid calcium-fortified orange juice, which often tastes chalky.

Coconut Cream: For every ounce of coconut cream you need, you can substitute ⅔ oz. coconut milk mixed with ⅔ oz. white sugar and a pinch of salt. Just be careful not to overdo it on the salt.

Cranberry Juice Cocktail: Most commercial cranberry juice isn't pure cranberry juice but cranberry juice *cocktail*, which is cranberry juice combined with other fruit juices and sweetened. It would be very unusual to have access to plain cranberry juice and **not** cranberry juice cocktail, but if you do, you can mix it with something like grape or cherry juice to taste, or just add sugar and water until it comes across as more sweet than tart. You may also want to add a touch of lemon juice to balance it.

Cream: Some of these recipes call for heavy cream, others for light cream or half-and-half. You can make something like half-and-half or light cream at home by combining heavy cream with whole milk in equal parts (or your preferred proportions). Directly substituting heavy for light cream or vice versa doesn't work quite as well, but it'll do in a pinch. Just add ½ oz. when switching from heavy cream to light, and take ½ oz. away when going in the other direction.

Crème de Cacao (Brown/White), Crème de Menthe (Green/White): I've specified white or brown crème de cacao in various recipes. This is always for color; in terms of flavor, they are interchangeable. The same goes for green and white crème de menthe. Note that the white versions are not actually white, but clear; and that other nondairy chocolate liqueurs can usually substitute for crème de cacao.

Crème de Cassis, Crème de Mûre: Made from black-currants and blackberries respectively, these can often be substituted for one another. The minimum allowable sugar content for crème de cassis is higher than it is for crème de mûre, so you may need to adjust the recipe to accommodate an increase or decrease in the liqueur's sweetness.

Curaçao or Triple Sec: Many other orange liqueurs can be used where curaçao or triple sec is called for. Just be careful with ones made on a brandy, tequila, etc. base instead of a neutral grain spirit base; they may play nicely with other kinds of liquor, but not necessarily.

Demerara Sugar/Syrup: Moscovado and turbinado sugar will give you similar flavor and texture to demerara in a simple syrup. Brown sugar will not work as well, but it'll be closer than white sugar. Alternatively, you can use maple syrup in place of rich demerara syrup; the sugar content will be about the same, and the flavor will be similar (if a bit more mapley).

Elderflower Liqueur: In addition to St. Germain and its imitators, there are nonalcoholic elderflower cordials on the market. They're usually European and will do as well in cocktails, although you may need to adjust the proportions depending on the sweetness of the cordial.

Grapefruit Soda: A Paloma made with fresh juice instead of soda isn't traditional, but it's tasty. Mixing ½ oz. grapefruit juice with ¾ oz. simple syrup and 3–4 oz. seltzer should put you in the ballpark. If you're feeling ambitious, make a grapefruit cordial (using the same method discussed above for the lime cordial) and mix ½ oz. of that with 3–4 oz. of seltzer.

High-Proof/Standard Proof Spirits: To substitute a spirit of about 40% ABV for one of about 50% ABV, use ¼ oz. more of the spirit than the recipe calls for. To do the opposite, use ¼ oz. less. This isn't a perfect solution—and it may not always be necessary—but if your drink doesn't seem quite balanced, give it a try.

Lemon Vodka: The traditional vodka for the Cosmopolitan is Absolut Citron, which is mostly lemon flavored with a hint of lime. You can infuse vodka with lemon fairly easily at home, but if you don't want a whole bottle of the stuff, you can approximate the taste in the Cosmo by using regular vodka and adding a large piece of lemon peel to the shaker.

Old Tom Gin: You can substitute Plymouth gin (preferable) or London dry gin (acceptable) in many recipes that call for Old Tom without doing too much damage. You can get a very rough approximation of how the drink would taste with Old Tom by also adding a teaspoon of simple syrup and a dash or two of orange bitters.

Port: In a pinch, you can substitute ruby for tawny port or vice versa.

Punt e Mes: Two parts of sweet vermouth and one part of your favorite amaro (Campari, Cynar, etc.) will approximate the flavor of Punt e Mes.

Raspberry Syrup: Raspberry preserves are sometimes used in place of raspberry syrup in cocktails. You can also use them to make an ad hoc syrup by mixing them with water (and sugar to taste, if necessary). Alternatively, you can always make other syrups from fresh fruit using the raspberry syrup recipe above or from fruit juice using the grenadine recipe; and ones made from similarly sweet-tart fruits like cranberries, redcurrants, and strawberries may make good substitutes in cocktails.

A Final Note

In case this section hasn't made it clear, none of the recipes in this book are written in stone. No recipe is or can be: tastes differ, palates evolve, ingredients change over time. Much like cocktails as a whole, each drink is a kind of canon unto itself. My goal in collecting these recipes has not been to give you the final version of any of them, but the first. Tinker with proportions, with ingredients, with structures—experiment and enjoy. I hope I've given you a solid, respectable place to begin.

Conversions

1 tsp. = ⅙ oz.

1½ tsp. = ¼ oz.

2 tsp. = ⅓ oz.

Juice of ½ lime = ~½ oz.

Juice of ½ lemon = ~¾ oz.

Juice of 1 lime = ~1 oz.

Juice of 1 lemon = ~1½ oz.

1 sugar cube = ~1 tsp. sugar

1 tsp. sugar has about the same sugar content as ¼ oz. of 1:1 simple syrup

1 tsp. 2:1 simple syrup has about the same sugar content as ¼ oz. of 1:1 simple syrup

⅙ oz. is *very close* to ⅛ oz.

⅓ oz. is consequently fairly close to ¼ oz., so you can use a scant 2 tsp. if you don't have a ¼ oz. measure

8 oz. = 1 cup = ½ pint

16 oz. = 2 cups = 1 pint

32 oz. = 4 cups = 2 pints = 1 quart

4 quarts = 1 gallon

⅕ gallon = ~750 mL

Beverage Glossary

Absinthe: A very high-proof (120°–150°) spirit traditionally flavored with wormwood, anise, and fennel. Intended to be substantially diluted with water before drinking, giving the spirit a hazy appearance as dissolved hydrophobic flavor chemicals clump together. Mostly used in small doses in cocktails. Not hallucinogenic, despite what you've heard.

Agave: A genus of succulents native to Mexico and nearby regions, from species of which mezcal and tequila are made (for which reason they are sometimes collectively termed **agave spirits**). The juice of agave plants may also be refined into a sweetener known as **agave nectar**.

Aged rum: : Rum that has spent any time aging in oak barrels. In this book, I have further distinguished among **lightly aged rum**, which is aged in oak barrels for 1–4 years; **filtered lightly aged rum**, a style typical of Cuba and Puerto Rico that is filtered after aging to remove the color; and **moderately aged rum**, which is aged 5–12 years. **Unaged rum** is surprisingly uncommon, but I have noted it as an option where I believe it works well.

Allspice Dram: A traditional Jamaican liqueur, made with a rum base and flavored with allspice. Also called **pimento dram.**

Amaretto: An Italian liqueur that tastes like almonds, although many traditional amaretti are in fact made from the pits of apricots or other stone fruits.

Amaro: A general term for bitter digestif liqueurs from Italy, increasingly also used to refer to similar products regardless of origin (such a spirit might otherwise be called a *bitter*—see **bitters**). The plural is *amari*. Noteworthy examples include **Campari**, described below, as well as the earthy **Amaro Nonino** and the artichoke-flavored **Cynar**.

Americano: A type of fortified wine flavored and bittered with gentian root. It's considered a subtype of *quinquina* by some sources and a wholly separate category by others; the truth is that the two *can* overlap, but don't necessarily. See **Kina apéritif wine**.

Apéritif or Aperitivo: Any beverage intended to open up the palate before food is consumed. Generally dry, light in body and alcohol, and mildly bitter, sour, or saline.

Apple Brandy: A spirit distilled from apples, normally aged in oak. Often called **applejack** in the U.S.; **calvados**, a French variety, is specified in some older cocktail guides. All three can be substituted for one another—just be sure you're using an actual apple brandy and not an apple-*flavored* grape brandy.

Aquavit: A Scandinavian spirit made like gin, but with dill and caraway as the preeminent botanicals rather than juniper. Also spelled "akvavit."

Bénédictine: A French liqueur with flavors of honey and baking spice.

Bitters: An infusion of herbs and spices in alcohol (or, occasionally, glycerin). Usually refers to *cocktail bitters*, like **Angostura** and **Peychaud's**. These are also called *non-potable* bitters, because the U.S. government considers them unpleasant to drink on their own and regulates them as grocery products rather than beverage alcohol. In this context, "bitters" is both singular and plural. *Potable bitters* are similarly produced but are considered beverage alcohol under U.S. law. All bitters are noticeably bitter in addition to their other flavors. See also **amaro**.

Black Rum: Rum that has been heavily colored, sweetened, and flavored after distillation, generally to evoke the character of molasses; reasonably considered a rum liqueur but rarely labeled as such. More viscous than unsweetened rums and useful in certain tiki-style drinks, especially in the case of funky and flavorful **Jamaican black rum**. Occasionally called blackstrap rum, but this is an imprecise term, because blackstrap molasses is commonly used in making rum whether or not it is subsequently colored or sweetened.

Bourbon: A type of American whiskey distilled from at least 51% corn and aged in new American oak barrels that have been charred on the inside. Most comes from Kentucky, but it can be made anywhere in the U.S. **Cask-strength bourbon** is not diluted at the time of bottling, usually leaving it around 55%–60% ABV.

Brandy: A spirit distilled from fruits, especially grapes. The fruit is generally specified, e.g., apple brandy, peach brandy, plum brandy; if none is given, grape brandy is implied. Aged brandy is assumed in cocktails unless otherwise specified, and Cognac is preferable if available. See **apple brandy**, **Cognac**, **kischwasser**, **pisco**.

Cachaça (kuh-SHAH-suh): A Brazilian spirit distilled from fresh-pressed sugarcane juice and bottled between 38% and 48% ABV. Cachaça available in the U.S. is usually unaged, but much of it spends at least a year in barrels made from oak or native Brazilian woods.

Campari: A brilliantly red Italian amaro bottled at 24% ABV. Quite bitter, with notes of citrus peel and sweet spice. Many products with like flavors are similarly colored, creating a category sometimes called **red bitter** or **Italian red bitter**. Note that this category also includes the lower proof but similarly flavored **Aperol** and *its* imitators.

Cane Syrup: Cooked, concentrated sugar cane juice. Retains a grassiness that is generally lost when the juice is further refined into crystalline sugar.

Chartreuse (shar-TROOZE): A brandy-based liqueur made by French monks according to a secret recipe with over one hundred ingredients. Comes in two varieties: the milder, 80° Yellow Chartreuse, and the bolder, 110° Green Chartreuse.

Cherry Heering: A Danish cherry liqueur aged in oak barrels, produced since 1818. Properly called **Heering Cherry Liqueur** and occasionally called **Peter Heering**, but Cherry Heering is the most common term.

Cognac: A type of brandy made in the French region of the same name, usually made from *ugni blanc* grapes and aged in French oak barrels. It is an ideal base for brandy cocktails and is often called for by name in old recipe books. "Cognac" is a contraction of *Cognac brandy* and should be capitalized.

Collins: A category of drink that is prepared in a tall glass with ice—rather than being shaken or stirred in a separate vessel—and then filled with seltzer. Meant to be drunk slowly as the ice melts and chills it, rather than quickly like a fizz.

Crème de [X]: A type of liqueur that contains at least 250 grams of sugar per liter (or 400 grams in the case of crème de cassis), which increases the viscosity and the perceived textural creaminess of the drink. Generally mixed or used in cooking rather than consumed on its own. "[X]" is the French name for the principal flavor; this book includes **crème de menthe**, **crème de cacao**, **crème de cassis**, **crème de mûre**, and **crème de violette**, which refer respectively to mint-, chocolate-, blackcurrant-, black-berry-, and violet-flavored liqueurs.

Curaçao (KER-uh-sow): Traditionally, a liqueur flavored with the peels of the *laraha* fruit, a bitter orange native to the Caribbean island of Curaçao, often made with a rum or brandy base and additional spices. Now commonly used to refer to orange liqueurs regardless of origin. Sometimes spelled "curacao" or "curacoa" in old cocktail books. See **triple sec**.

Demerara Sugar: A less-processed form of sugar that retains more of the flavor and characteristics of molasses than white sugar does. Useful for adding richness to cock-tails, and sometimes for making rum. **Turbinado sugar** and **muscovado sugar** are similar products with different degrees of processing.

Digestif or Digestivo: Any beverage meant to seal off the palate after a meal and, traditionally, to aid in digestion.

Usually strongly flavored, higher proof than an apéritif, and noticeably bitter and sweet.

Dry: In describing an alcoholic beverage, the opposite of sweet. May imply astringency.

Falernum: A low-proof Caribbean liqueur with a rum base, traditionally flavored with ginger and baking spices, and often with accents of nuts and lime. Sometimes available as a nonalcoholic syrup.

Fassionola: A tropical fruit punch syrup with a passion fruit base. Traditionally came in natural, red, and green varieties, with lime added to the green and cherry to the red. Modern recipes often feature more complex fruit blends. Red or natural fassionola (the latter sometimes written *passionola*) will work in a Hurricane, but I particularly recommend the red variety from Cocktail & Sons.

Fizz: A category of drink that is shaken to chill and then topped with seltzer without the addition of ice. Intended to be drunk quickly, like a shorter cocktail, rather than lingered over, like a **Collins**.

Flip: A category of drink that is shaken with a whole egg. Generally served cold and dusted with nutmeg.

Fortified Wine: A wine to which distilled spirits have been added. Often also *aromatized*, or flavored with herbs and spices, and generally sweeter than ordinary wine. **Port** and

sherry are fortified wines, while **vermouth** and **quin-quina** are both fortified and aromatized.

Galliano: A yellow Italian liqueur with a pronounced vanilla flavor and notes of cinnamon, mint, and anise, made according to a secret recipe.

Gin: A spirit distilled like vodka and additionally flavored with juniper and other complementary botanicals, either by infusion or by vapor extraction during distillation. London dry gin should be assumed if a type is not specified. See also **London dry gin**, **Old Tom gin**.

Ginger Ale: A sweet soda with a mild ginger flavor. A more robustly flavored or alcoholic version is generally called **ginger beer**.

Grenadine: A syrup made from pomegranate juice and sugar, occasionally with distilled spirits or citrus accents added. In the United States, the term is commonly used for red-flavored corn syrup, but the word comes from the French for *pomegranate*, "*grenade*," and this is the essential flavor in cocktails that call for grenadine.

Irish Whiskey: A type of whiskey made in Ireland, generally either distilled from barley or made by blending barley whiskey with a whiskey distilled from other grains. Usually lacks the peat-smoke flavor of Scotch.

Kina Apéritif Wine: Not a standard industry term, but used in this book to refer to any fortified and aromatized wine considered an acceptable substitute for the discontinued quinquina Kina Lillet. Its descendant, Lillet Blanc, is not a good substitute in traditional recipes; neither are other prominent quinquinas like Dubonnet and Byrrh, which are usually called for by name in cocktail recipes rather than by category. The best replacements are newer quinquinas that include "Kina" in the brand name to telegraph their purpose, and **Cocchi Americano**, which is confusingly both a quinquina *and* an americano. See also **quinquina**, **americano**.

Kirschwasser: An unaged brandy distilled from cherries. It is used as an accent in cocktails, and appears as a base spirit only rarely. Often shortened to **kirsch**.

Lime Cordial: Preserved sweetened lime juice, developed as an antiscorbutic for use by the British Royal Navy. The most flavorful ones incorporate lime oils from the peels or leaves in addition to the juice and sugar. Accept no substitutes in a Gimlet.

Liqueur: A product made by sweetening a distilled spirit and flavoring it, generally with fruits, spices, or both. Often but not always bottled at less than 40% ABV, with the 15%–30% ABV range often called **liqueur strength**. The base is usually a neutral distillate, but it is not uncommon for it to be brandy, and other spirits are used from time to time.

London Dry Gin: The most common type of gin for cocktail use, and heavy on citrus and juniper; no flavors may be added after distillation. Interestingly, London dry gin may be made anywhere in the world. **Plymouth gin** is a closely related style and a reliable alternative.

Maraschino Liqueur: A liqueur made by sweetening a distillate of marasca cherries, traditionally produced on the Dalmatian coast.

Martini: A cocktail comprising gin (or vodka, if specified), dry vermouth, a lemon twist or cocktail olive, optionally orange bitters, and not one other godforsaken thing.

Mezcal: A spirit distilled from agave in certain regions of Mexico, especially Oaxaca. Its production process involves exposure to smoke over several days, which often imparts flavor to the finished spirit. Because the majority of mezcal is **joven**, or unaged, it is generally distinguished by the agave varietal used, **espadin** being the most common. Mezcal can be made from any type of agave, including blue agave (although this is uncommon). See also **tequila**.

Neutral grain spirit: See **vodka**.

Old Tom Gin: A type of gin with a higher viscosity than London dry, due to added sugar, barrel aging, or both.

Popular in the nineteenth century and revived in the first decade of this one.

Orange Flower Water: A suspension of aromatic particles in water, made either by steeping blossoms of the bitter orange in water or as a byproduct of essential oil distillation.

Orgeat: A traditional French syrup made from almonds, generally accented with orange flower water or other floral or citrus components. Pronunciation of this word is agreed upon by no one. Personally, I favor "or-ZHAH."

Pastis: A French spirit flavored with anise. Lower in strength (generally bottled at 40%–50% ABV) and less herbaceous than absinthe, but commonly used as a substitute while the latter was banned.

Pimm's No. 1 Cup: An English gin-based liqueur flavored with fruit. Higher-numbered Pimm's Cups made with whiskey, brandy, and rum used to exist, but have been discontinued.

Pisco: A grape brandy produced in Peru and Chile (and the national spirit of both). Peruvian pisco may not be aged in oak, while Chilean pisco can be but isn't necessarily; unaged pisco should be assumed unless otherwise specified.

Port: A fortified wine originating in Portugal. The fortification occurs before fermentation is finished, leaving some of the natural sugars behind. Comes in two varieties: the drier, aged **tawny port** and the sweeter, younger **ruby port**.

Proof: A measurement that corresponds to twice the percentage of ethanol in a spirit, which may be indicated using the degree sign (°) – e.g., a 45% ABV spirit could be described as ninety proof or 90°, both vocalized the same way. In this book, a **standard-proof** spirit is in the ballpark of 80°, a **high-proof spirit** is in the ballpark of 100°, and an **overproof spirit** is appreciably higher, in the 130°–150° range. Recipes should be assumed to call for standard-proof spirits unless otherwise specified.

Punt e Mes: A bottling of two parts sweet vermouth and one part amaro, considered a type of vermouth in the **vermouth con bitter** style.

Quinquina: A type of fortified and aromatized wine flavored with quinine and other spices. **Dubonnet**, **Byrrh**, and the defunct **Kina Lillet** are all examples, but are not reliable substitutes for one another. See also **Kina apéritif wine**.

Rhum agricole: A style of rum made from fresh sugarcane juice, which often has savory or grassy notes not found in other rums. Typical of areas historically under French influence; **Martinique rhum agricole** is particularly lauded. Similar products from other regions are often labeled as **cane juice rum.**

Rum: A distilled spirit made from sugarcane or its derivatives, including cane juice, sugar, and molasses. Normally aged in oak barrels after distillation and sometimes filtered after aging to remove the color. In this book, I have avoided the imprecise terms light, white, or silver rum, which can refer to either a filtered rum or an unaged one; gold or amber rum, which can refer to either an unfiltered aged rum or an unaged rum that has been lightly colored; and dark rum, which can refer to either an aged rum or a rum that has been heavily colored and sweetened. See instead **aged rum**, **black rum**, and **rhum agricole.**

Rye Whiskey or **Rye:** A type of American whiskey distilled from at least 51% rye grain and aged in oak barrels. Traditionally associated with the mid-Atlantic states.

Scotch: A type of whisky made in Scotland, generally exposed to peat smoke during its production, which may give an earthy, smoky taste to the finished spirit. Particular flavors are associated with the whiskies from certain regions of Scotland, including the especially smoky and peaty **Islay Scotch**. A **single malt Scotch** is distilled from 100% malted barley at a single distillery; a **blended Scotch** combines a single malt with other Scottish whiskies, whether single malts from other distilleries or whiskies distilled from other grains. Blended Scotch is assumed in cocktails unless otherwise specified. "Scotch" is a contraction of *Scotch whisky*, and should be capitalized.

Seltzer: Carbonated water to which nothing else has been added. **Club soda** is carbonated water with mineral salts added to imitate the flavor and texture of naturally occurring (and often naturally carbonated) **mineral water**. **Soda water** or **sparkling water** can refer to any of these. While distinct in flavor, other carbonated waters are usually satisfactory replacements for seltzer in cocktails.

Sherry: A Spanish fortified wine, aged using a *solera* system whereby new wine is added to existing aging stock in a barrel as some of the old mixture is drawn off. The major varieties, from dry to sweet, are **fino**, **manzanilla**, **amontillado**, **palo cortado**, and **oloroso**. **Cream sherries** have been additionally sweetened, usually by blending with sweet wines. All sherry recipes in this book are tailored to **amontillado**, which is a good middle-of-the-road option for cocktails.

Sparkling Wine: A wine that has been carbonated through either fermentation or the direct addition of carbon dioxide gas. In cocktails, a dry sparkling white wine should be assumed. The gold standard is **Champagne**, made according to traditional methods in that region of France; American sparkling wines, as well as Spanish **cava** and

Italian **prosecco**, can also work well in cocktails and are frequently less expensive.

Tequila: A spirit distilled from blue agave in one of five regions of Mexico, especially Jalisco. Classified by how long it's aged in oak: not at all for **blanco**, 2–12 months for **reposado**, and 1–3 years for **añejo**. **Mixto tequila** is a blend of 51% tequila with 49% neutral grain spirit; it's the kind that gave you terrible hangovers in college, and is called for nowhere in this book.

Triple Sec: A liqueur flavored with orange peels, usually with a more neutral spirit base than curaçao. French in origin, but now commonly used to refer to any sort of orange liqueur regardless of provenance. See **curaçao**.

Vermouth: A fortified and aromatized wine, traditionally flavored and bittered with wormwood and other spices. The two most important styles in cocktails are **dry vermouth**, also known as **French vermouth** or **Marseilles dry vermouth,** which is pale in color and contains up to 40 grams of sugar per liter; and **sweet vermouth**, also known as **Italian vermouth**, which is red and contains up to 150 grams of sugar per liter. Less common in the U.S. but very popular internationally is a clear semisweet style called **blanc** or **bianco vermouth**. Open bottles of vermouth should always be refrigerated.

Vodka: A spirit distilled from *anything*, generally until it is as close to pure ethanol as Nature allows, then blended with water until it reaches a potable strength. Known as **grain alcohol** or **neutral grain spirit(s)** if not diluted.

Whiskey: A class of distilled spirit made from cereal grains, most commonly barley, corn, and rye. Almost always aged in oak barrels after distillation. Spelled "whisky" for products from Scotland, Japan, and Canada. See also **bourbon**, **Irish whiskey**, **rye whiskey**, **Scotch**.

Bibliography

Amann, Kirsten, and Misty Kalfoken. *Drinking Like Ladies.* Beverly, MA: Quarry Books, 2018.

Arnold, Dave. *Liquid Intelligence.* New York: W. W. Norton, 2014.

Berry, Jeff. *Beachbum Berry Remixed.* San Jose, CA: SLG Publishing, 2010.

Billstein, Kelli. "The Art of the Meal." *Saveur*, Apr. 7, 2014.

Bradford, Luke. *Abacus.* Published by the author, 2018.

Bruni, Frank. "Smitten With a Cocktail Called Frisco." *The New York Times*, Oct. 28, 2010.

Cate, Martin, with Rebecca Cate. *Smuggler's Cove.* Berkeley, CA: Ten Speed Press, 2016.

Civil, Miguel. "Modern Brewers Recreate Ancient Beer." Chicago University Oriental Institute News and Notes, no. 132 (Autumn 1991): 1–4.

Choong, Kim. "Jungle Bird—The True Facts." *ThirstMag.com*, Feb. 25, 2020.

Cotton, Leo, edited by Jonathan Pogash, with Rick Rodgers. *Mr. Boston Official Bartender's Guide: 75th Anniversary Edition.* Hoboken, NJ: John Wiley & Sons, Inc., 2012.

Craddock, Harry. *The Savoy Cocktail Book.* London: Pavilion Books, 2011.

Difford, Simon. "Future Classic Cocktails." *Difford's Guide*, Sep. 6, 2019.

Embury, David. *The Fine Art of Mixing Drinks.* New York: Mud Puddle Books, 2009.

English, Camper. "The History of Grenadine Use in Cocktails: Literature Review." *Alcademics*, Dec. 18, 2012.

———. "What's the Difference Between Orange Curacao and Triple Sec?" *Alcademics*, Feb. 21, 2011.

———. "Paloma History - Tracing the Facts and Fiction about this Tequila Cocktail's History" *Alcademics*, Nov. 28, 2017.

"Falernum Files: A Q&A with Richard Seale." *The Sugarcane Press*, Nov. 11, 2018.

Fleming, Ian. *Casino Royale*. London: Penguin Books, 2002.

Ford, Doug. "The Diamondback Cocktail." *Cold Glass*, Mar. 7, 2015.

Greene, Philip. *To Have and Have Another*. New York: Perigee Books, 2012.

Haigh, Ted. *Vintage Spirits and Forgotten Cocktails Deluxe Edition*. Beverly, MA: Quarry Books, 2009.

Kosmas, Jason, and Dushan Zaric. *Speakeasy*. Berkeley, CA: Ten Speed Press, 2010.

MacElhone, Harry. *Barflies and Cocktails*. Paris: Lecram Press, 1927.

Meehan, Jim. *Meehan's Bartender's Manual*. California and New York: Ten Speed Press, 2017.

———. *The PDT Cocktail Book*. New York: Sterling Epicure, 2011.

Mennies, Leah. "Can Boston's Only Classic Cocktail Make a Comeback?" *PUNCH*, Nov. 25, 2015.

Morgenthaler, Jeffrey. "I Make the Best Amaretto Sour in the World." *JeffreyMorgenthaler.com*, Feb. 9, 2012.

Munro, Lizzie. "Mastering the Clover Club with Julie Reiner." *PUNCH*, Sep. 16, 2016.

Parsons, Brad Thomas. *Bitters: A Spirited History of a Classic Cure-All*. Berkeley, CA: Ten Speed Press, 2011.

Petraske, Sasha, with Georgette Moger-Petraske. *Regarding Cocktails*. New York: Phaidon Press, 2016.

Pietrek, Matt, and Carrie Smith. *Minimalist Tiki*. WonkPress, 2019.

Schorow, Stephanie. *Drinking Boston*. Boston: Union Park Press, 2012.

Simonson, Robert. *A Proper Drink*. Berkeley, CA: Ten Speed Press, 2016.

———. "The Rise and Fall of the Aviation Cocktail." *PUNCH*, Dec. 7, 2017.

Sutcliffe, Theodora. "Ngiam Tong Boon." *Difford's Guide*, undated.

Wondrich, David. *Imbibe!* New York: Penguin Group, 2015.

Acknowledgments

A lot of people helped me test recipes for this book, even after COVID-19 prevented us from doing so in person. Thank you to Jason Adams, Denise Alfonso, Ozair Ali, Nick Andersen, Alyssa Bilinski, Alan Bishop, Luke Bradford, John Brewer, Steve Corman, Christopher Ell, Caroline Fenn, Anna Flores-Amper, Carlos M. Greaves, Nick Groh, Brian Lagoda, Oren Lurie, Luke Massa, Sam Meyer, Michael Mitchell, Matt Mitterhoff, Reed Morgan, Ayesha Nishtar, Rachel Orol, Liz Palazzolo, Cristina Ruiz, Clare Sachsse, Leah Libresco Sargeant, Maria Schwarz, Richie J. Suffling, Kyle Torres, Tristyn Wade, Steffi Weinraub, and Andrea Zurita, for helping make sure that people besides me would like these recipes! Particular thanks to Alexander Rodion Michaud, for his helpful feedback on my writing as well as on the cocktails.

My thanks as well to those who helped me with other research, including Kelli Billstein, Eric Felten, Lee Morgan, Bob Sennett, Fred Yarm, and especially Camper English and Matt Pietrek.

Thanks to David Fabricant, for inviting me back to take on this project; and to my editor, Lauren Bucca, and everyone else at Abbeville Press, for making this book a reality.

To Shannon Fabricant, thank you for personally causing my writing career. To Molly Jarvis, thank you for giving me the right cocktail book at the right time to get me started in hospitality. To my parents, thank you for indulging my nontraditional professional path.

Finally, a very big thank you to Elizabeth Aslinger, whose palate shaped this book more than any other taster's, and whose liver bore the brunt of the recipe testing after COVID-19.

SELECTED TINY FOLIOS™ FROM ABBEVILLE PRESS

- *American Impressionism* 978-0-7892-0612-1
- *Ansel Adams: The National Park Service Photographs*
   978-0-7892-0775-3
- *Audubon's Birds of America: The National Audubon Society
   Baby Elephant Folio* 978-0-7892-0814-9
- *The Art of Rock: Posters from Presley to Punk* 978-0-7892-0611-4
- *The Art of Tarot* 978-0-7892-1306-8
- *Fashion: Treasures of the Museum of Fine Arts, Boston*
   978-0-7892-1380-8
- *Frank Lloyd Wright: America's Master Architect* 978-0-7892-0227-7
- *New York: Treasures of the Museum of the City of New York*
   978-0-7892-1361-7
- *Norman Rockwell: 332 Magazine Covers* 978-0-7892-0409-7
- *Treasures of the Addison Gallery of American Art* 978-0-7892-0758-6
- *Treasures of the Art Institute of Chicago: Paintings from
   the 19th Century to the Present* 978-0-7892-1288-7
- *Treasures of the Brooklyn Museum* 978-0-7892-1278-8
- *Treasures of Impressionism and Post-Impressionism: National
   Gallery of Art* 978-0-7892-0491-2
- *Treasures of the Museum of Fine Arts, Boston* 978-0-7892-1233-7
- *Treasures of the National Museum of the American Indian*
   978-0-7892-0841-5
- *Treasures of the New-York Historical Society* 978-0-7892-1280-1
- *Women Artists: National Museum of Women in the Arts*
   978-0-7892-1053-1

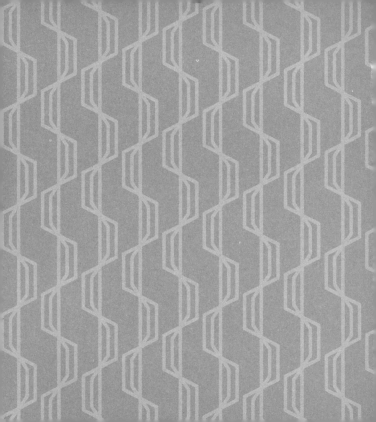